Contemporary
COOKING

Volume 1

Contemporary
COOKING

Volume 1

3M

Contemporary Cooking

Editorial production by James Charlton Associates, Ltd. New York. Editor-in-Chief, James Charlton; Managing Editors, Barbara Binswanger, Jennie McGregor; Food Editors, Inez M. Krech, Cecile Lamalle, Anne Lanigan, Maria Robbins.

Book production and manufacturing consulting by: Cobb/Dunlop Publishing Services, Inc., New York Art Direction and interior design by: Marsha Cohen/Parallelogram

Acknowledgments: Pat Cocklin, Delu PAL International, Alan Duns, John Elliott, Melvin Grey, Gina Harris, Anthony Kay, Paul Kemp, David Levin, David Meldrum, Roger Phillips, Nick Powell, Iain Reid, John Turner, Paul Williams, Herbert Wise, George Wright, Cuisinarts, Inc.

Printed and bound in Yugoslavia.

Library of Congress Cataloging in Publication Data
Main entry under title:

Contemporary Cooking.

  Includes index.
  1. Cookery. I. Minnesota Mining and Manufacturing Company.
TX715.C7586   1984   641.5   84-2563
0-88159-500-4 — (set)
ISBN: 0-88159-000-2

CONTENTS

for the Contemporary Cooking Series

VOLUME 1

Part One — 1

APPETIZERS, SOUPS, EGGS, CHEESES, SAUCES

In this volume STOCKS AND SOUPS

Part Two — 27

POULTRY, MEAT, FISH, SEAFOOD

In this volume BROILING POULTRY, MEAT AND FISH

Part Three — 53

BREADS, GRAINS, PASTA, FRUITS, VEGETABLES

In this volume GREEN SALADS

Part Four — 79

DESSERTS, CAKES, COOKIES, PASTRY

In this volume CAKES

Part Five — 103

ENTERTAINING

In this volume AUTUMN ENTERTAINING

INDEX — 112

Part One
STOCKS AND SOUPS

When you are weary, cold and hungry, what is more comforting, more soothing, more nourishing and more restorative than a bowl of steaming, homemade soup? Is there a kinder, truer friend in all the world of food than soup? Soup cools in summer, warms in winter. A poor man's soup—potatoes, leeks and water—is as delicious in its way as the most elegantly garnished *consommé double* served at a rich man's dinner. There is a Spanish proverb that unabashedly declares, "of soup and love, the first is best," and Lewis Carroll went on at length about the joys of soup, concluding rapturously, "Beautiful soup! Beautiful soup! Soup of the evening, beautiful, beautiful soup!"

Ever since man discovered a way to heat water over fire, soup has been an important part of our diet. In his *Dictionary of Gastronomy*, André Simon says, "Through the ages soups have played a role similar to bread. As a basic food every country, every civilization has had its soup: France its *pot-au-feu*; Italy its *minestrone*; Russia its *borscht*; China its sharks' fin soup; Britain its brown or Windsor soup; the United States its black bean soup; Switzerland its gravy soup; and Scandinavia, its fruit soups."

The connection between soup and bread is linguistic as well as traditional. The word soup is linked to the Germanic *sop*—sop is the bread over which broth is poured—and it appears to be connected to the Latin *suppa* as well. If there is soup and there is bread, then there is supper.

In European peasant households nothing is wasted, no food is ever thrown away. Leftover bread is sliced and dried and to this very day French farming families begin their evening meal with soup (*panade*)— their bowls half filled with crusty day-old bread, then covered with steaming soup of the day. The famous onion soup from France is a more elaborate, sophisticated version of this same idea.

There is a charming folktale about a clever cook who makes a tasty soup from water and a stone. A hungry traveler appears one evening on the doorstep of a stingy peasant woman. He has a magic stone, he tells her. The stone will make a soup if she will let him use her pot. He boils some water and the stone, takes up a spoonful of the soup and making loud noises of appreciation, tells her that only a pinch of salt, perhaps an onion, could possibly improve the broth. The woman is entranced. He gets some salt, an onion, and tastes the soup again . . . Only a few potatoes, a little cabbage, could make it any better. The woman's appetite is whetted, her curiosity as well, and she supplies the vegetables. He tastes again and rolls his eyes in ecstasy—the soup is utterly delicious . . . Only a hint of pork, the smallest piece of ham, would do it justice.

Of course the soup was good. The silly woman bought the stone for quite a lot of money and the traveler ate well, took to the road again, secure in his abilities to make another soup with whatever ingredients he laid his hands on. Many people enjoy making soup precisely because the recipes are flexible, the process is relaxed, and there is ample room for inventiveness and creativity.

Like most good things, soup is of humble origin and for centuries soup making thrived in poor people's kitchens. In 1765, in Paris, a man named Boulanger had a good idea. He decided to sell bowls of soup in his shop on Rue Bailleul. He set up a few tables and hung out a sign declaring his soups to be *restaurants,* i.e., restoratives. "Boulanger," he claimed, "sells magical restoratives." His motto, inscribed in Latin above the entrance, invited the public to, *"Venite ad me omnes qui stomacho laboratis et ego restaurabo."* (Come to me all of you whose stomachs cry out and I will restore you.) The idea caught on and the rest is history.

By the nineteenth century soup had become chic and soup making was considered the ultimate accomplishment of a chef. Auguste Escoffier declared that, "Of all the items on the menu, soup is that which exacts the most delicate perfection and the strictest attention, for the success of the rest of the dinner depends largely on the impression, good or bad, that it has produced on the guest."

And the great chef Antonin Carême stated baldly that, "I cannot understand a dinner without it. I hold soup to be the well beloved of the stomach."

As the great chefs incorporated soups into their repertory, they transformed the simple, homey, peasant broth into refined and subtle preparations. Their recipes grew more elaborate, requiring equipment and ingredients to be found only in the wealthiest houses and most exclusive restaurants. But there evolved, as well, some basic principles and a vocabulary that we still use in writing recipes for making soup.

Soups are generally divided into two broad categories—clear soups and thick soups. Among the former you will find *stocks, broths, bouillon* and *consommé.* There is much confusion in the use of these terms and you will often find them used interchangeably, but it will simplify things to remember that they are all essentially the same and that the difference between one and another results from the amount of reduction and the strength of flavor.

Stocks are called *fonds de cuisine* in French, meaning "foundations of cooking," and so indeed they are. A stock is made by simmering meat, aromatic vegetables, herbs and a variety of seasonings, slowly and for a long time, until all the goodness and flavor have been extracted. The process cannot be hurried, and "simmering" is the key word. Alexandre Dumas called this simmering of the stock, *"faire sourire le pot-au-feu,"* in other words, the successful cook is the one who is able "to make the pot smile." After 4 to 5 hours of careful simmering and skimming, the liquid is strained and possibly further reduced to concentrate the flavor. In the end, the stock is clear, every bit of fat has been removed, and it may be stored in the freezer to be used in making other soups, a wide variety of sauces, as well as stews and gravies. A cook who has a freezerful of stock is like a man with money in the bank.

Broths (the word is related to *brew*) are generally made in the same way, but usually the cooking time is not as long, and the ingredients—meat, vegetables, pasta and grains—are not discarded, but rather served along with the flavored liquid.

Various "boiled dinners" such as the Italian *bollito misto,* corned beef and cabbage, and even Cock-a-Leekie, are prototypes of hearty broths or whole-meal soups.

Bouillon is simply the French term for stock or broth and usually refers to a clear soup that can be eaten on its own as well as being used as an ingredient in other dishes.

A consommé is thought by some to be the queen of soups. It is a stock that has been enriched, concentrated and clarified. Full-bodied flavor, smooth texture, rich color and sparkling clarity are the key factors. It is the perfect opening to a formal dinner and it is often enriched by the addition of a fortified wine—a fine old sherry, Madeira or even port.

Various soups are made from seafood, among them the famous fish soup-stews such as the *bouillabaisse* of southern France and Italy's *cacciucco.* Fish stock is prepared along the same principles as meat stock but cooking time is very short. Often the fish is poached in a light, quickly cooked vegetable stock called *court bouillon.* True to its name, a court bouillon is quickly made by simmering water or wine, a little lemon juice or vinegar, a shallot and some herbs. The Japanese *dashi* is yet another delicate infusion, based on kelp and dried bonito shavings. It is made quickly, not even simmered, but brought to a boil, removed from the heat and then allowed to steep.

Among the thick soups you will find purées and cream soups. Purées are simple, nourishing soups, usually vegetables cooked in a stock or milk or water. When all the vegetables are done, the soup is puréed. A food mill or a sieve work very well but a blender or food processor is even easier. Cream soups are richer versions of the same, or they are thickened with a roux and then enriched with egg yolks, cream and butter.

There are many other routes to soup making, and today a great international array of soups is part of the American cook's heritage. From Spain comes the versatile gazpacho, whose best-known American version consists of sliced or chopped raw vegetables turned into a kind of liquid salad by the addition of oil and vinegar, thinned with water, wine, or (rarely) stock.

Another family of soups worth discovering are the fruit soups (blueberries, raspberries, apples and sour cherries) of eastern Europe and Russia. They are often served cold, and are extremely refreshing in summer. The repertoire of cold soups in this part of the world extends much farther than fruit soups. The flavorful *Kaltschalen* (cold bowls) of Germany and the related Scandinavian cold soups are often based on sour cream, sour milk or buttermilk, with sugar and cinnamon; sour black bread, beer, wine and lemon juice are among the other favorite ingredients. To the east, cold soups made or garnished with soured milk products are equally popular in the Baltic States and Russia. The best known in this country is cold borscht, which is delicious when made from fresh young beets and thinned with buttermilk or sour cream.

There is nothing quite like the flavor of all-from-scratch soups. And one big reason for the recent renaissance in the ancient art of soup making is that more and more cooks are discovering that one need apply only the humblest kitchen skills to produce something that appeals both to sophisticated palates and to the contemporary appetite for down-to-earth food.

STOCK

Stock is a liquid food made by cooking various combinations of ingredients slowly to extract all their flavors and nutrients. Stocks made from meats and poultry are cooked for hours, fish and vegetable stocks usually for no more than an hour.

Stock is seldom used by itself; rather it makes the basis for soups, sauces, aspics, casseroles; it can also be used for fat-free pan cooking for low-calorie diets. Since it is cooked further in these dishes, it is essential that stock be only lightly seasoned and flavored; salt should be omitted altogether or used sparingly.

White stocks are made from chicken or turkey, veal or rabbit, or combinations of these. The meats are not browned. Chicken is the best all-purpose choice; it is delicate but flavorful. Lamb and pork are strong-tasting and suitable only for dishes made with those meats; ham and other cured meats are too salty.

Brown stocks are made from beef, veal, chicken and game, alone or in combination, but the bones and meats are browned before being cooked in liquid.

Fish stock is made from heads, bones and trimmings of fish, especially cod, flounders, snappers, grouper, striped bass. The heads are most valuable since they release gelatin, which is protein, to the stock, making more nutritious and flavorful stock and *fumet*. Wine is often used as part of the liquid because it helps to speed dissolving of gelatin from the fish bones.

The vegetables used for flavoring stock are those favorites of good cooks: celery, carrots, onions and leeks. Do not use beets or tomatoes since they color the stock, and do not use any strong-flavored vegetable such as turnip or members of the cabbage family, as these develop an unpleasant taste through long cooking.

Vegetable stocks use the same cooks' favorites, plus mushrooms, lettuce leaves, and peas. Potatoes are not used as they would cloud the stock. Broths can be made of a single vegetable, especially celery and mushrooms, to be used for special recipes.

Stock can be made with bones alone, and they are the most important ingredient. Have your butcher crack them so that the marrow can enrich the stock. However, you will have more flavorful results if some meat is used in addition to bones.

Bouquet Garni

1 Collect a sprig of fresh thyme, a few sprigs of fresh parsley and a bay leaf.

2 Tie herbs together with white string or strong cotton thread, leaving a long end which can be tied to stockpot handle.

 OR If using dried herbs, except parsley, place them on a square of muslin or cheesecloth.

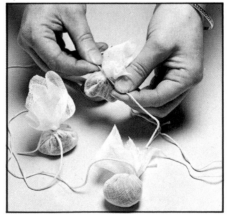

2 Gather edges of cloth together and tie tightly into a small bag, leaving a long end of string or thread.

Preparing Ingredients for Stock

Have meats cut into chunks and bones cracked or chopped. They may be used without further preparation, but you will have a clearer and more flavorful stock if you blanch or parboil these basic ingredients before starting. This will minimize the scum that rises in the early stage of cooking. The blanching process is essential for veal bones and knuckles and is recommended for chicken pieces or whole fowl:

Put bones in the stockpot, cover with cold water, and bring to a rapid boil.

When the ingredients have boiled for 5 minutes, drain and rinse bones, discard water, and clean stockpot.

Return bones to the cleaned pot and add any additional meats.

Vegetables and fresh herbs for stock should be washed and dried.

Remove any damaged portions of vegetables and cut them into a few large pieces.

It is not necessary to scrape carrots, but they must be well scrubbed.

Do not remove leaves from celery ribs, as they add flavor.

Leeks are essential for stock; cut off roots, pull off any damaged outer layers, and split the leeks lengthwise. Wash very carefully to remove all sand between the layers.

Onions need to be peeled; if large they should be halved.

Fresh herbs can be tossed into the stockpot with the vegetables but, as we so seldom have all fresh herbs, it is more usual to collect them in a *bouquet garni*. There are three ways to do this:

If you have mostly fresh herbs, tie them together with white string. Keep a length of the string tied to the handle of the stockpot; it is easy to retrieve at the end of cooking.

If you have dried herbs, collect them on a square of cheesecloth or thin muslin and tie it closed. These little bags may float freely in the stock or may be tied to the handle.

The usual herbs for the *bouquet garni* are parsley (fresh gives the best

Brown Stock

Makes 5 cups

5 pounds meaty beef bones, shin or marrow, cracked, rinsed
    vegetable oil, as needed
2 large onions
3 large carrots
2 celery ribs
12 cups cold water, or as needed
1 bouquet garni
6 peppercorns
    salt

• Another way to brown the meat and bones is in the oven. Preheat oven to 350°F. Arrange the meat and bones in one layer and roast in the oven until they are golden brown. This will take approximately 1 hour. Add the vegetables for the last 30 minutes.

• You can control the darkness of your stock by the amount you roast the meat and vegetables. The darker they are, the darker the stock. Take care, however, not to burn them.

1 Sauté bones and meats in a heavy pan over low heat until fat is extracted.

2 Increase heat slightly; cook until meats and bones are well browned. Add oil, if needed. Stir to brown evenly.

3 Meanwhile, prepare the vegetables and cut them into large chunks.

4 Add vegetables to bones and meats and cook until they become golden in color. Continue from step 2 of white stock.

White Stock

Makes 5 cups

5 pounds veal knuckles
2 onions
3 large carrots
2 celery ribs
1 large leek
12 cups cold water, or as
   needed
1 bouquet garni
6 peppercorns
   salt

1 Cut vegetables into chunks. Put into stockpot with blanched meat and bones, preferably veal.

2 Add cold water to the pot and bring very slowly to a boil.

• Have butcher crack the veal knuckles. Blanch them in boiling water for 5 minutes. Scrub or peel all the vegetables.

• White stock may also be made from chicken parts, turkey parts, breast of veal, and any other scraps of veal you may have saved.

• It is definitely worthwhile to save up bits of poultry, scraps of veal and bones. Store them in the freezer until you have enough to make a stock.

• Feel free to improvise. No leeks? Use another onion, a couple of shallots, even scallions. The final result will still be every bit as good.

• The best stocks are made with fresh ingredients. However, carcasses of roasted poultry and game can be used to make stock that is flavorful, even if less nutritious.

• Many cooks add vegetables only after scum has stopped rising in large quantities, but as long as stock is skimmed carefully, vegetables can be added at the outset.

• White stock is an essential ingredient for cream soups, fine white sauces and delicate aspics. It is an excellent all-purpose stock to have on hand.

• White stock is flavorful for cooking rice, barley and almost every other kind of grain.

5 Half-cover the pot and simmer for 4 to 5 hours.

6 Continue to skim as needed; add boiling water if liquid falls below level of solid ingredients.

OR If time allows, let the stock cool, then skim off the fat with a skimmer or large spoon.

OR If you have more time, let stock cool completely and refrigerate until fat solidifies on the surface. Lift it off.

3 As scum rises to the surface, carefully lift it off with a skimmer or large spoon.

4 When scum has stopped rising in large quantities, add bouquet garni and seasoning (remember to use a light touch with salt).

7 Pour stock through a colander into a clean pot or large bowl. Or ladle it through the colander.

8 If stock is needed at once, blot fat from the surface with kitchen paper towels.

9 Strain degreased stock through a sieve lined with dampened muslin or through several layers of cheesecloth.

10 If stock lacks flavor, simmer to reduce and concentrate it. Season to taste.

flavor and is available year-round), thyme and bay leaf. Rosemary and marjoram, cloves and peppercorns, are sometimes added. These are pungent, so use sparingly. Also avoid using ground herbs, as they tend to cloud stock.

Another simple way to assemble the flavoring herbs is to put them all in a stainless steel tea infuser; this is easy to retrieve when stock is done.

Bouquet garni may be used in soups, sauces, casseroles, even in some baked dishes, so it is a useful kitchen trick to know.

Fish Stock

The procedure for this is slightly different, since fish releases its protein and flavor so much more quickly than does meat.

Use only raw fish parts, and be sure they are fresh.

Cover with cold water and stir, then drain at once.

Discard solids and filter the stock.

For standard stock, use 2 pounds of heads and bones and 2 quarts of water.

For stronger stock *(fumet),* use 4 pounds heads and bones. If you use wine, a good proportion is 1 cup wine to 4 cups water. If you do not wish to use wine, add the juice of 1 lemon.

Break up the large pieces. Put them into the stockpot with all other ingredients and simmer for 30 minutes after liquid reaches the boiling point.

Completing Stock

As a stock cooks there will be some evaporation of the liquid, which is desirable as it is by means of this reduction that the flavors are concentrated. However, liquid should not fall below the level of the solids; if it does, the heat may be too high. Add boiling water if necessary to cover the solids.

When stock is completed, pour or ladle it through a colander set in a clean pot or large bowl. It is better to

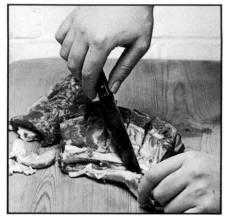

1 Rinse bones under cold running water. Cut away as much fat as possible.

2 Put bones and meat in a large stockpot or heavy saucepan and cover with cold water.

3 Bring slowly to a boil. Using a skimmer, lift off scum and fat as they rise to the surface.

4 Add salt (sparingly) and barley if used. Cover the pot and simmer gently for 30 minutes.

5 Thoroughly scrub or peel vegetables and cut them into 1-inch dice.

6 Add vegetables to the pot, at intervals according to the time needed to cook them. Continue simmering for 1½ hours.

7 Turn off heat. Lift bones and meat from broth; discard bones and cut meat into pieces.

8 Blot up any remaining fat from the surface with paper towels.

9 Return meat pieces to the broth, reheat to serving temperature, garnish and serve.

ladle, as a heavy pot of near-boiling liquid is awkward to handle.

If time allows, cool the stock, then refrigerate it. The fat will rise to the top and become solid; it can then easily be removed.

If you need stock at once, let it rest long enough for fat to rise to the surface, then carefully blot it up with paper towels. Now stock is ready to be filtered. Pour it through a fine sieve lined with moistened muslin or cheesecloth, or use a paper coffee filter.

Taste the stock; if it seems to lack flavor, bring it again to a boil and cook until reduced to strenghten concentration. Some cooks advocate boiling for reduction, but simmering is preferred for better flavor. If you are preparing brown stock and it seems to lack color, this can be adjusted by adding a tiny bit of meat glaze, available under various names. However, if the stock is not brown enough, the reason is that the meats were not browned sufficiently. When you make the next batch, you can solve that problem.

Storing Stock

It is best to store stock without additional seasoning; that way you will always have a supply ready for any use; the specific seasoning or additional flavoring for some particular dish can be done when you are ready to use the stock.

After stock is strained, degreased, filtered, and reduced if necessary, let it cool, then transfer it to covered glass jars and refrigerate.

If you do not plan to use the stock within 4 days, freeze it at once, allowing headspace in the jars (stock expands as it freezes). It is most convenient to freeze it in 1- or 2-cup jars; larger amounts take too long to defrost.

When solidly frozen, be sure jars are tightly closed; if in doubt, overwrap the jar tops with clear plastic. Label and date the jars.

Meat and poultry stocks can be stored in a refrigerator-freezer for 2 months, in a separate freezer kept at 0°F for 4 months. Defrost stock in the refrigerator overnight, then bring it to a boil before using it.

Fish stocks must be refrigerated. These must be used within 1 day, or should be frozen. They can be stored in a refrigerator-freezer for 1 month, in a separate freezer at 0°F for 2 months. Bring defrosted stock to a boil at once before using it.

Vegetable stocks or broths should be used within 2 days, or should be frozen. They can be safely stored for 6 weeks in a refrigerator-freezer; in a separate freezer they can be stored for 3 months. Bring defrosted stock to a boil at once before using it.

Hearty broths

Hearty broths are soup-stews that can make a meal-in-a-bowl. Broth made with water requires the same sort of long slow cooking as stock. The liquid must be skimmed carefully, then the meat should be cooked until partly tender. Other ingredients are then added, first those that require longest cooking, last the most tender foods. Already cooked foods or leftovers can be used in these broths, and very small amounts of vegetables.

Gentle simmering will give you a soup with distinct pieces of ingredients; rapid boiling will break up the pieces.

The second method will thicken the soup somewhat, especially if potatoes are used. In addition to vegetables, grains (rice, barley) and pasta (bowknots, shells) may be added; dumplings can be steamed on top of the solids.

While these broths are not thickened with flour or an egg-cream liaison, they may be thickened with added vegetable purées; or part of the vegetables in the broth may be puréed and returned to the soup.

If the pieces of meat or poultry contain bones, lift them out when the broth is done. Separate meat and bones and cut meat into bitesize pieces.

If broth is fatty, spoon off as much as possible, then blot up the rest with paper towels. Return meat pieces to soup and reheat to serving temperature.

You can make broths based on your own homemade stock. Simply bring stock to a simmer and add the ingredients in order.

If raw meats are used, add them first.

If cooked meats are used (diced meats or sliced frankfurters), add them last, for heating to serving temperature is all they need.

Dried legumes (beans, peas, lentils) that have been presoaked and root vegetables require the longest cooking time.

Other vegetables may need only minutes; do not overcook them, for you want their texture and taste in these broths.

Grains and pasta may be cooked separately, to be added at the end. Pasta releases starch, which can cloud the broth. Barley releases quite a bit of scum. However, if cooked separately, they will add no thickening at all to the broth, so do whatever suits your purpose.

Consommé

Consommé is the final refinement of stock. It must be crystal-clear, well-flavored, and have the right color for its type. Once you have made a good stock, consommé is easy.

If you are making stock for the purpose of consommé, be sure to have meat as well as bones for a more intense flavor. Some of the bones should be gelatinous—a veal knuckle or a pig's foot is a valuable addition, and essential if you plan to jelly the consommé.

Wine may be added, and it helps speed release of the gelatin. Fortified wines (sherry, port, Madeira, etc.) are best added toward the end if this is a flavor touch you want, as long cooking will diminish the flavors, but table wines

Clarified Beef Consommé (Consommé Double)

4 portions

3 pounds lean meaty beef bones
   vegetable oil as necessary
1 pig's foot or veal knuckle
2 Spanish onions
1 large carrot
2 celery ribs
2 teaspoons sugar
½ cup Marsala, sherry or red wine
8 cups water, or as needed
1 bouquet garni
1 bay leaf
⅛ teaspoon salt
6 peppercorns

Second cooking
6 ounces lean beef
1 carrot
1 celery rib
1 medium-size onion
   grated rind of 1 orange
2 egg whites and shells

Final flavoring
   salt and pepper
2 sprigs of marjoram
1 sprig of rosemary
3 tablespoons Marsala, Port or Madeira

• Have the beef bones cracked and the pig's foot split or the veal knuckle cracked. Peel or scrub vegetables, trim, and cut into small chunks.
• For second cooking, use beef cuts such as sirloin or top round, boneless and very lean. Beef may be chopped, ground, or cut into thin slices.
• Beat the egg whites just enough to mix them, and crush the shells. (For larger amounts of stock, more egg whites will be needed.)
• For perfectly transparent consommé, it is essential to filter the stock through several layers of dampened cheesecloth or muslin.
• The final flavoring of wine should be added as you reheat the consommé for serving.

1 Sauté meaty bones in large soup pot until evenly browned, about 15 minutes. Add a little oil, if necessary, to prevent sticking.

2 Add pig's foot or veal knuckle, vegetables, sugar; stir until sugar caramelizes. Add wine and water. Bring to a boil; skim.

5 Chop beef, carrot and celery for second cooking. Peel onion, blanch for 2 minutes, then quarter and chop.

6 Add beef, vegetables, orange rind, egg whites and shells to degreased stock. Whisk over medium heat until boiling.

9 Season the consommé to taste. Pour it again through a sieve lined with a double layer of dampened cheesecloth into a clean saucepan.

10 Degrease the consommé. Add the herb sprigs, cover, and simmer for 30 minutes. Cool. Discard herbs and degrease again.

3 Reduce heat; add bouquet garni, bay leaf, salt and peppercorns. Simmer, partially covered, for 4 hours. Add boiling water if needed.

4 Strain stock through a colander lined with cheesecloth. Chill. Degrease by removing surface fat. Pour stock into a clean pot.

7 Egg white will form a foamy layer on top. Stop whisking, reduce heat, and simmer uncovered for 1 hour.

8 Very slowly pour the contents through a sieve lined with a double layer of cheesecloth and set over a large bowl.

11 To serve hot, reheat the consommé and add the wine. Ladle into warm bouillon cups and garnish as desired.

12 For jellied consommé, refrigerate cold soup for 4 to 8 hours. Chop jelly; spoon into chilled glass bowls; add lemon garnish.

should be added early so that the alcohol can evaporate and the flavor can blend with the other ingredients.

Beef or game consommé should start with browning, as in making brown stock, to give good color. Chicken or veal for consommé may be browned or not.

Another trick to add color is to brown the stock vegetables in a little oil, or a mixture of oil and butter. When they are lightly browned, sprinkle them with granulated sugar and continue to cook them, stirring. The sugar will caramelize and brown and will add a rich color.

For simple or single consommé, completed stock—strained, defattened and filtered—is clarified.

A double consommé has double cooking and double flavoring. As with single consommé, it starts out with good stock, strained, degreased and filtered.

Puréed Soups

Puréed soups are simply cooked vegetables or fruits, puréed with their cooking liquid. With the blender or food processor, it is easy and quick to complete them. Only a little more work is required if they are puréed through a food mill or sieve.

Root vegetables, tubers and legumes will give a thick purée without added ingredients, but watery vegetables should be cooked with potatoes or other starchy addition to give the right texture to the purée. The liquid used can be vegetable cooking water reserved from other recipes, or it can be plain water, or plain chicken or other white stock.

Wash and trim vegetables; if you plan to put them through the food mill they need not be peeled. Slice or chop them.

They can be put in the liquid directly, or for a slightly richer soup they can be precooked in butter and/or oil, a process that develops flavor through cooking the natural sugar in the vegetables. This is a sort of

12

braising; the cooking term is "sweating" since the only moisture in the pan is the natural moisture of the vegetables and this is slowly extracted by the heat.

Heat the butter and/or oil in a heavy soup pot and add the vegetables; stir them gently to coat with fat; then cover with a sheet of buttered foil with a tiny hole in the center for escape of steam. Let them cook for 10 to 20 minutes, according to texture of the vegetable.

Remove foil and pour in the liquid. Add seasoning.

Bring to a simmer and cook until vegetables are completely tender. Purée in batches in a blender or a food processor fitted with the steel blade. Or put through a food mill.

Combine all the batches of purée and reheat to serving. You may turn the purée into a cream soup by adding sweet or sour cream, or enrich it with the addition of butter.

Some good vegetables for puréed soup are carrots, peas, potatoes, tomatoes, zucchini, winter squashes including pumpkin, and celery knob. Good combinations are onion and cauliflow-

er, spinach, sorrel or watercress with potato; leek and potato; onion and potato.

Dried Beans

Dried beans and peas require a bit of extra care. Delicious soups are made from dried black beans, white beans, red beans, garbanzos, split peas and lentils. It is no longer necessary to soak beans overnight. Sort the beans to remove any stray pebbles, rinse, and cover with water. Bring to a boil and keep boiling for 1 minute. Turn off the heat,

Puréeing Vegetable Soup

1 Melt butter in a heavy pan. Add prepared vegetables, cover, and sweat gently over low heat for 5 to 10 minutes.

2 Season lightly and add liquid. Cover pan and simmer for 15 to 25 minutes, until the vegetables are tender.

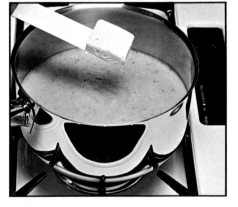

3 Set food mill over a bowl or another saucepan and turn handle until vegetables are puréed.

OR Set a conical sieve over a bowl or another saucepan and press vegetables through the sieve.

OR Pour liquid and vegetables, part at a time, into a blender container or a food processor, and purée them.

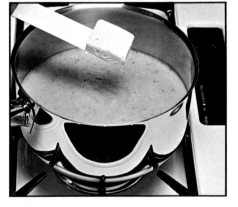

4 Combine all batches of purée and reheat gently over low heat. Adjust seasoning. Do not let purée boil.

cover, and let rest for 1 hour. Then cook according to the recipe. Beans should cook over low heat and at a gentle simmer. Never salt them until they are quite tender and almost ready to eat. Salt will make them tough. Most beans should cook for as long as 4 to 5 hours. Peas and lentils take less time. Add seasonings and aromatic vegetables during the last hour of cooking.

Garnishing Soups

All soups can be served with a garnish, from something as simple as minced fresh parsley or grated lemon rind to something as elaborate as pastry puffs. Some garnishes for consommé include julienne strips of orange rind; pancake strips or squares; shredded greens such as sorrel and tender lettuce, which have been blanched for 1 minute and well drained. All puréed vegetable soups can be garnished with tiny florets or slices of the vegetable; these are also good on cream soups, hot or cold. Some good examples of garnishes are julienne strips of carrot, celery, green or red pepper; paper-thin slices of cucumber, mushroom or lemon; watercress sprigs; snipped chives; swirls or whipped sweet or sour cream; grated cheese. Split almonds sautéed in butter, or other nuts chopped or grated; shelled whole tiny shrimps or split or chopped shrimps, or tiny lobster or crab claws or crayfish legs; slivers of chicken or other meats. Float garnishes on the soup just before serving; or serve them in separate bowls.

Fresh croutons also make an attractive garnish for many soups. Add just before serving for a crunchy texture that is irresistible.

Croutons step-by-step

Makes 2 cups

4 slices of firm bread
1½ ounces unsalted butter
1 teaspoon vegetable oil

• Although white bread is most traditional for croutons, any good-quality bread will do. Experiment with whole wheat, rye, pumpernickel.

• Sauté a garlic clove along with the bread cubes for just a hint of garlic flavor.

 **1** Stack the slices and trim off crusts.

 **2** Cut bread into ½ inch cubes.

 3 Melt butter with oil in a heavy pan. Add bread cubes.

 **4** Sauté for about 2 minutes, turning to brown the cubes evenly.

 **5** Remove croutons with slotted spoon; drain on paper towels. Serve or keep warm in low oven until ready to serve.

Chicken Stock

3 quarts

1	stewing chicken, 5 to 6 pounds, with giblets	1	leek
1½	pounds veal knuckle, cracked	1	celery rib
2	large carrots	12	cups cold water, or as needed
2	onions	1	bouquet garni
		6	peppercorns
			salt

Cut chicken into pieces. Set liver aside for another use (liver clouds the stock). Put chicken, giblets except liver, and veal knuckle in a large stockpot. Scrub carrots and cut into pieces. Peel and quarter onions. Wash leek carefully, and slice it. Slice celery. Add all vegetables to the stockpot and pour in enough water to cover ingredients by 2 inches. Bring slowly to a boil. Skim constantly to remove all scum. Add *bouquet garni* and peppercorns. Reduce heat to a simmer and let the stock cook for about 4 hours. Add more water as necessary to keep ingredients covered.

Pour the whole stockpot of ingredients through a colander into a clean pot. Discard the solids (although the chicken can be used for sandwich spreads or fillings). Now pour the stock through a large sieve lined with a double layer of moistened cheesecloth. Add salt only at this point. Refrigerate the stock for up to 3 days or freeze for up to 2 months. Boil stored stock before using.

Vegetable Stock

3 cups

¾	pound vegetable peels and trimmings (celery ribs, water cress or parsley stems, carrot and tomato peels, mushrooms stems, green leaves of leeks)	3	white peppercorns
		1	bouquet garni
		4	cups water
			salt

Rinse vegetable pieces and put in a large saucepan. Add peppercorns, *bouquet garni* and water. Bring to a boil and simmer for 30 minutes to 1 hour. Pour through a colander into a clean saucepan. Press solids with the back of a wooden spoon to extract all liquid. Strain stock through a sieve lined with moistened cheesecloth. Add salt to taste only now; or add salt when you are ready to use the stock.

Fish Stock

2 cups

1½	pounds fish bones and trimmings, including heads and rib portions	3	cups cold water, or as needed
1	onion or leek		juice of 1 lemon
1	celery rib	1	bouquet garni
1	cup white wine	2	peppercorns
			salt

Rinse fish trimmings and put into a large stockpot. Peel and slice onion or leek; slice celery. Add to the stockpot with wine, water, lemon juice, *bouquet garni* and peppercorns. Bring the liquids to a boil, then reduce to a simmer and cook for 30 minutes.

Pour through a colander into a clean saucepan; discard solids. Strain stock through a sieve lined with a double layer of moistened cheesecloth. Taste. If stock is not strong enough, simmer to reduce it and concentrate flavor. Add salt only now, or when you plan to use the stock. *Note:* For a fish stock that is to be jellied, be sure to add rib portions and heads as they will release more natural gelatin.

Consommé Rosé

4 portions

1½ pounds ripe, firm tomatoes
4 cups chicken consommé
2 celery ribs with leaves

5 ounces canned pimientos
  salt and pepper
2 tablespoons chopped fresh
  parsley

Blanch and peel all the tomatoes. Set aside one third of them for garnish. Chop the rest of the tomatoes. Pour consommé into a large saucepan and add chopped tomatoes and celery ribs. Simmer for 30 minutes, until tomatoes are reduced to a pulp. Pour the soup through a strainer lined with a double layer of dampened cheesecloth. Press with a wooden spoon to get as much of the tomato pulp as possible.

Chop the tomatoes for garnish, and discard the seeds. The pieces of tomato should be about the size of a dried lentil. Drain the pimientos and rinse to remove any seeds. Cut pimientos into thin strips. Divide chopped tomatoes and pimiento strips among 4 soup bowls. Reheat strained consommé to serving temperature, season to taste, then pour into soup bowls. Sprinkle each serving with parsley.

Scotch Broth

6 portions

1½	pounds neck of lamb, with bones	3	small leeks	
7	cups cold water	2	small white turnips	
1	teaspoon salt	1	onion	
2	ounces pearl barley	2	celery ribs	
3	small carrots		black pepper	
		2	tablespoons minced fresh parsley	

Chop the bones, if butcher has not done it, and cut off and discard as much fat as possible. Put bones in a soup kettle, add the cold water, and bring slowly to a boil. Use a flat skimmer to lift off scum and fat as they rise to the surface. Continue skimming until all scum has been removed. Add salt and barley, cover the kettle, and simmer for 30 minutes.

Wash the vegetables carefully, scrape or peel them, and cut into 1-inch pieces. Add vegetables to the broth, cover the kettle, and simmer for 1½ hours longer.

When broth is done, lift out all the bones with a slotted spoon and let them cool for a few minutes. With 2 forks, detach the meat from the bones and shred it. Discard bones, fat and gristle. Remove as much surface fat from the broth as possible, blotting it up with absorbent paper towels.

Return the meat to the kettle and reheat soup to serving temperature. Add black pepper to taste and more salt if needed. Sprinkle each serving of soup with some minced parsley.

Soupe au Pistou
(Provençal Vegetable Soup)

6 portions

	Pistou (Basil and Garlic Paste)	4	large garlic cloves
2	cups fresh basil leaves, no stems	3	ounces Parmesan or Romano cheese
		½	cup olive oil

Soup

8	ounces fresh shell beans	1½	pounds zucchini
1	pound fresh green snap beans	8	cups water
1	pound potatoes	2	tablespoons olive oil
2	medium onions		salt and pepper
3	medium carrots		fresh or dried savory and rosemary (optional)

First make the *pistou.* This keeps well in refrigerator or freezer, so prepare the whole amount, even if not all is needed for the soup. In a food processor chop the basil and garlic; add the cheese and continue until cheese is grated and the mixture puréed. Pour in the olive oil, little by little, until the mixture is a smooth green paste.

Wash and drain shell beans. Top and tail snap beans, wash, and cut into 2-inch lengths. Peel and chop potatoes, onions and carrots. Wash and trim zucchini, but do not peel them. Chop into large pieces. Pour the water into a large kettle and bring to a boil. Heat the oil in a large skillet and in it sauté the onions until golden. Add zucchini and sauté for a few minutes more. Turn the vegetables and remaining oil into the kettle of water and add shell beans, snap beans, potatoes and carrots. Bring to a boil, then simmer for about 1 hour, until all vegetables are tender and the soup flavorful. Season with salt and pepper about halfway through the cooking, and add a few pinches of the Provençal herbs—savory and rosemary—if you like. Spoon the *pistou* into the soup just before serving; use as much as you like. Or spoon a little into each serving, about 1 teaspoon.

Note: Other vegetables such as cabbage, celery, tomatoes, Swiss chard can be added to the soup. All the vegetables may be sautéed in oil before being added to the soup kettle.

Avgolemono

Greek Egg and Lemon Soup

2 portions

2   **cups chicken stock**
¼   **cup cooked rice**
1   **large egg**

2   **tablespoons fresh lemon juice**
    salt and pepper

Pour chicken stock into a saucepan and add the rice. Bring to a slow simmer. Beat egg and lemon juice together and add salt and pepper to taste (if stock is salted, use very little salt). Stir a ladle of hot broth into the egg mixture to warm it, then turn it into the rest of the soup. Simmer to serving temperature; do not let the soup boil. Serve at once.

Oriental Chicken and Mushroom Soup

6 portions

2 ounces dried Chinese
   mushrooms
4 cups chicken stock
6 ounces cooked white meat
   of chicken

   salt and pepper
4 tablespoons dry sherry
4 tablespoons minced
   watercress

Soak dried mushrooms in hot water to cover for 20 minutes. Lift out mushrooms, rinse, and dry. Filter the soaking liquid and set aside. Discard mushroom stems (they are tough) and slice the caps. Pour stock into a saucepan and add mushroom soaking liquid. Bring to a boil. Cut the chicken into thin slivers and add it and the mushroom slices to the stock. Simmer for 5 minutes. Season to taste. Add sherry. Ladle into warmed soup cups and garnish with watercress.

Stracciatella

4 to 6 portions

4½ cups chicken stock
2 tablespoons grated
   Parmesan cheese

2 large eggs

Bring stock slowly to a boil. Put grated cheese into a bowl and break eggs on top of cheese. Stir vigorously with a fork or whisk until cheese and eggs are well blended.

As soon as stock reaches the boiling point, pour in the egg and cheese mixture in a thin stream, stirring the stock all the time to break the egg into strands (rags is the literal meaning of the Italian name). Remove soup from heat and serve immediately.

Billi-Bi
(Mussel Soup)

6 portions

4 pounds mussels in shells	1 ounce unsalted butter
2 cups dry white wine	3 shallots
1 small onion	3 cups light cream
1 garlic clove	salt and white pepper
6 parsley sprigs	cayenne pepper
2 celery ribs with leaves	

Scrub mussels and remove beards. Discard any with broken or open shells. Cover mussels with water in a large kettle and let them soak for 5 minutes. Lift out mussels and discard soaking water. Rinse kettle; be sure no sand remains. Return mussels to the kettle and pour in the wine. Peel and halve onion and garlic and add to kettle. Separate parsley stems and leaves; mince leaves and set aside for later. Add stems and celery ribs to the kettle. Bring wine to a boil, cover the kettle, and steam mussels, turning them halfway through, for about 5 minutes, until all shells are opened. Discard any shells that have not opened. Remove mussels from shells, turning any juices into the kettle. Reserve the mussels for a salad or first course; they are not used in the soup. Strain the steaming liquid through a coffee filter or through a fine sieve lined with a triple layer of moistened cheesecloth.

Melt butter in a large saucepan. Peel and mince shallots and sauté them in the butter until tender. Stir in the reserved minced parsley and sauté for 1 minute. Pour in the filtered mussel liquid and the light cream. Simmer for 5 minutes. Season with salt and white pepper to taste. To serve hot, heat to serving temperature; to serve cold, chill for several hours. Sprinkle with a pinch of cayenne pepper.

Tunisian Chick-pea Soup

6 portions

8 ounces dried chick-peas	3 cups canned peeled tomatoes
4 cups water	juice of 1 lemon
1 carrot	1 teaspoon salt
1 bay leaf	cayenne pepper
1 onion, stuck with 2 cloves	1 red bell pepper
3 tablespoons olive oil	3 sprigs of fresh coriander
1 garlic clove	
1 teaspoon whole cuminseeds	

Cover chick-peas with water and soak them overnight. Next day, lift peas to a colander and rinse them. Discard soaking water. Put soaked peas in a kettle and add 4 cups water. Scrape carrot and halve it. Add carrot to kettle with bay leaf and onion. Bring to a boil, then simmer very gently for 1 hour, until chick-peas are very soft. Lift out and discard carrot pieces, bay leaf, and onion. Set aside the kettle of chick-peas.

Heat oil in a large saucepan. Peel garlic and put through a press into the oil. Crush the cuminseeds in a mortar and add to the oil. Let garlic and spice cook over low heat for 2 minutes, then add tomatoes and simmer for 20 minutes. Combine tomato mixture with chick-peas and any remaining cooking liquid, then in batches purée the soup in a food processor or through a food mill. Return soup to the saucepan and add lemon juice, salt, and cayenne pepper to taste (in Tunisia they like the soup hot). Reheat slowly to serving temperature. Meanwhile, trim red pepper and dice it; mince coriander. Serve the soup with pepper and coriander as garnishes.

Carrot and Watercress Soup

4 portions

8 ounces carrots	3½ cups chicken stock
1 small onion	salt and pepper
1 bunch of watercress	4 tablespoons dairy sour
2 tablespoons corn oil	cream

Scrub and scrape the carrots; peel the onion. Grate both in a food processor or with a hand grater. Wash and trim the watercress; discard about half of the stems (they can be bitter). Chop the watercress and set aside about 3 tablespoons for garnish. Heat the oil in a large saucepan and add the vegetables. Cook over low heat, turning vegetables often, for about 10 minutes. Vegetables should be soft. Pour in the stock, bring to a boil, cover, and simmer for about 20 minutes.

Purée the soup in a blender or food processor, or put through a food mill. Return to the saucepan and heat to serving temperature. Season to taste. Spoon soup into 4 bowls. Drop 1 tablespoon sour cream on each bowl and swirl it around in a spiral. Sprinkle reserved chopped watercress on top.

Zuppa alla Pavese

4 portions

2 ounces unsalted butter	4 large eggs
4 slices of French bread	4 cups beef consommé
3 tablespoons grated Parmesan cheese	

Melt the butter in a skillet and sauté the bread slices in it until golden on both sides. Place a bread slice in each of 4 heated soup bowls. Sprinkle bread with cheese. Break 1 egg into each soup bowl so that it falls to one side of the bread slice, not on top of it.

Heat the consommé to boiling, then ladle it gently over the egg and bread. The hot consommé will cook the egg just enough.

Variation: For consommé Friar Tuck, beat 2 large egg yolks with 3 tablespoons heavy cream. Pour into boiling beef consommé through a sieve.

Celery and Walnut Soup

4 portions

½	cup walnut pieces	4	tablespoons flour
1	cup milk		salt and pepper
2	cups chicken stock	2	large egg yolks
1	small onion	½	cup heavy cream
2	celery ribs	2	tablespoons chopped
1	ounce unsalted butter		walnuts for garnish (optional)

Chop nuts in a nut grinder or food processor. Scald the milk in a saucepan. Add walnuts to milk and let stand, covered, for 20 minutes. Heat stock to a simmer. Peel and mince onion. Trim celery and cut into ½-inch pieces. Melt butter in a heavy saucepan over low heat; add onion and sauté for 3 minutes. Add celery and sauté for 2 minutes. Stir in flour and cook for 3 minutes, stirring all the while. Pour in heated stock and milk with walnuts. Stir over low heat until mixture is smooth and thickened; continue to simmer for about 15 minutes. Purée the soup in a blender or food processor, or push through a food mill. Return to the saucepan and season with salt and pepper.

Beat eggs and cream together. Pour some of the hot soup into the liaison to warm the eggs, then turn the liaison into the rest of the soup. Simmer the soup over low heat for about 4 minutes. When the first bubble appears to indicate the soup is nearly boiling, remove from heat. Garnish with chopped walnuts.

Cock-a-Leekie

6 portions

18	large prunes	2	celery ribs
1	stewing chicken, 4 to 5 pounds	1	bouquet garni
			salt and pepper
10	cups water	3	tablespoons chopped fresh parsley
7	leeks		

Pit the prunes. Put them in a saucepan with enough cold water to cover. Bring to a boil, remove from heat, and set aside, covered, until cool.

Cut chicken into 8 pieces and put in a stockpot with the cold water. Bring to a boil, skimming often to remove fat and scum. Reduce to a simmer and cook for 1 hour. Meantime, wash leeks thoroughly, trim, and cut both green and white parts into slices. Trim celery and cut into ½-inch pieces. Add vegetables, *bouquet garni,* and a small amount of salt and pepper to the chicken. Simmer, partially covered, for 50 minutes longer. Drain prunes and add to the pot. Continue to cook until chicken is about to fall from the bones. Remove soup from heat and transfer chicken to a plate.

When chicken is cool enough to handle, remove skin and bones and cut meat into small pieces. Remove surface fat from soup and discard *bouquet garni.* Return chicken to the pot and reheat to serving temperature. Correct seasoning. Sprinkle with parsley and serve.

Beef Soup with Herb Dumplings

6 portions

6	cups beef stock		1	celery rib
2	onions		6	ounces cooked boneless
1	large potato			beef
4	carrots			salt and pepper

Dumplings

1¼	cups all-purpose flour		½	teaspoon crumbled dried
1½	teaspoons baking powder			tarragon
½	teaspoon salt		1	tablespoon minced fresh parsley
½	teaspoon crumbled dried		1	egg
	thyme		½	cup milk, or as needed

Bring beef stock to a simmer in a large saucepan. Peel and chop onions and potato. Scrape, trim, and slice carrots. Trim and slice celery. Cut beef into ½-inch pieces. Add vegetables to stock and simmer for 5 minutes.

Meanwhile, prepare dumplings: Mix flour, baking powder, salt and herbs together in a bowl. Beat egg and milk together, and slowly stir into the flour to make a stiff dough. Add more milk if necessary.

Add beef pieces to the stock. Drop the dumpling batter by tablespoons into the simmering stock. Cover and let the soup simmer for about 10 minutes. When the dumplings are cooked, they will float. Serve the soup piping hot.

Chinese Hot and Sour Soup

4 portions

2 ounces dried Chinese mushrooms
3½ cups beef stock
1 tablespoon soy sauce
½ teaspoon Chinese hot sauce
salt and pepper

4 ounces boneless beef round
4 ounces canned bamboo shoots
4 green onions (scallions)
1 ounce (2 tablespoons) Chinese rice wine or sherry

Soak the mushrooms in hot water to cover for 20 minutes. Lift out mushrooms, rinse, and pat dry. Filter the soaking liquid and set aside. Discard mushroom stems (they are tough) and slice the caps. Bring stock to a boil. Add soy sauce, Chinese hot sauce, the filtered mushroom liquid, and salt and pepper to taste. Remove saucepan from heat.

Use a sharp knife to cut the beef into very thin strips. Drain bamboo shoots and cut into small pieces. Trim green onions and cut into slivers.

Bring stock again to a boil, add the beef, reduce heat, and simmer for 5 minutes. Add bamboo shoots and green onions and simmer for 4 minutes longer. Remove soup from heat, stir in rice wine, and serve immediately.

French Onion Soup

6 portions

12	ounces yellow onions			salt and pepper
3	ounces butter or margarine		6	thick slices of French bread
5	cups well-flavored beef stock		4	ounces Emmental cheese
1	bay leaf		1	ounce Parmesan cheese

Peel the onions and chop fine, by hand or in a food processor. Melt butter or margarine in a heavy saucepan. Add onions and cook over low heat, stirring often, until onions are translucent and beginning to brown. Add stock and bay leaf. Cover the pan and simmer for 30 minutes. Taste soup, and add seasoning as needed.

Toast bread slices lightly on both sides. Grate both cheeses and mix together.

Remove and discard the bay leaf and pour the soup into an ovenproof tureen or into 6 individual heatproof bowls. Drop a slice of bread into each bowl and cover with a thick layer of the grated cheeses. Put the tureen or the bowls into a preheated 400°F. oven and cook for 10 to 15 minutes, until cheese is melted and sizzling. Serve soup at once.

Leek Soup

4 portions

1 pound leeks
1 ounce unsalted butter
1¼ cups chicken stock

1¼ cups milk
salt and white pepper
2 tablespoons natural yogurt

Wash leeks carefully; trim root ends and discard any damaged leaves; cut off raggedy ends of green leaves, but keep as much of the green part as possible. Slice leeks into rings. Cover with cold water, bring to a boil, simmer for 2 minutes, then with a slotted spoon lift leeks out to a colander. Rinse and drain. Discard the blanching water.

Melt the butter in a heavy pan and sauté the leeks in it for 2 minutes. Add chicken stock and milk, cover, and simmer for 30 minutes. Do not let the mixture boil, just simmer.

Purée the soup in a blender or food processor, or put through a food mill. Reheat to serving temperature. Taste, and add salt and pepper. Stir in the yogurt and serve.

Variations: For onion soup, substitute onions for leeks. For carrot soup, use 1 pound carrots and 2 onions in place of leeks. For lettuce soup, use 1¼ pounds lettuce and a small onion in place of leeks.

Orange and Tomato Soup

4 to 6 portions

1 large potato
1 medium-size onion
2 large oranges
¼ to ½ cup chicken stock or
    water
1 ounce unsalted butter
3½ cups canned peeled
    tomatoes

1 tablespoon tomato purée
1 bay leaf
    pinch of dried rosemary
    pinch of salt
    black pepper
3 tablespoons grated
    Parmesan cheese
    (optional)

Peel potato and onion and cut into small pieces. Wash and dry the oranges. Grate the orange rind and set rind aside. Squeeze juice from the oranges and pour into a measuring cup. Add as much stock as needed to fill the 1-cup measure.

Melt the butter in a large saucepan over moderate heat. Add potato and onion and simmer until onion is translucent. Pour in the orange juice and stock mixture, the tomatoes and

tomato purée. Add bay leaf, rosemary, salt and a little black pepper. Bring to a boil and simmer for 40 minutes. Purée the soup through a food mill, then return it to the rinsed saucepan. Stir in the orange rind. Taste and add more seasoning if necessary. Reheat soup to serving temperature. Sprinkle each portion with a little grated cheese, if you like the flavor.

Part Two

BROILING POULTRY, MEAT AND FISH

Broiling is one of the oldest methods of cooking, and still one of the finest for certain foods. Yet it is often treated rather cavalierly by cooks, both those who tend to ignore it because it is so simple and those who rely on it all the time for the same reason. The diner who goes into a fine restaurant and orders a plain broiled steak or chop may be regarded with pity by those intent on ordering the craze of the season—but on the other hand, he may be alert to the truest test of the kitchen's mettle.

Broiling is virtually the same technique as spit-roasting, and what can be said about one can be said with only minor adjustments about the other. Both undoubtedly go back to the first discovery of how to roast meat on a stick over a fire. Both are dry-heat methods involving intensely high temperatures that seal in flavors under a browned crust; in some regards both are still at their best when practiced under fairly primitive circumstances over an open fire or bed of coals. In spit-roasting the food revolves to expose all surfaces; in broiling it remains stationary to the heat source. By an unfortunate circumstance of language the word "roast" is usually applied in modern cookbooks to the baking of meat in ovens—an excellent method, but not the same as spit-roasting.

Toasting bread is a kind of broiling, and until this century bread was usually toasted by holding it on a fork in front of the fire. Make the experiment with a good fire, and if you are lucky enough not to drop the bread in the flames you will see that a fine fire imparts something that the best electric toasters do not. The same is true of meat cookery; most of us do our best with gas or electric oven broilers, but an occasional hearth-broiled steak makes us wonder what we are missing. The gap is partly filled by the technique known as panbroiling, in which the food to be cooked is placed directly on a very hot dry surface—the best being the ridged cast-iron pans that keep melting fat from the surface of the meat.

Some kinds of meat are better suited than others to the techniques of broiling and roasting—understood here to mean spit-roasting. Nor are these methods equally admired in all cultures and cuisines. They are almost entirely foreign to the spirit of Chinese cooking, which has traditionally been geared to making the most of scarce fuel resources.

The Japanese, despite their own historic fuel scarcity, reserve the highest admiration for broiled foods (called *yakimono*). Beef did not enter their cuisine until the nineteenth century, and even now is an extremely expensive luxury. But fish—virtually the only animal-protein source known on the Japanese islands for centuries—is perfect for broiling with limited fuel, since it takes only a few minutes to cook through. "Salt-broiling" *(shioyaki),* in which the fish is sprinkled with salt before broiling, creates an especially fine and crisp effect, since much of the moisture in the fish is drawn off by the salt. The skin quickly takes on a roasted flavor, while the smaller bones become brittle and crunchy enough to be eaten, with a wonderfully savory effect. All kinds of seafood are frequently threaded on small skewers for broiling, and the arrangement of food on skewers for optimum presentation of cooking surfaces is a carefully thought-out skill far removed from our often haphazard shish kebab cookery.

The home of true shish kebab is, of course, the Middle East, where the most common meat is lamb. As it happens, lamb is probably the best suited of all meats for broiling and spit-roasting. Lamb—and to some extent mutton, the meat of mature sheep—have enough internal reserves of fat and moisture to keep basting themselves from within, while many cuts are also free enough of fiber to be tenderized rather than toughened by cooking.

By contrast, veal cannot stand up to the intensity of most dry-heat cookery. True spit-roasted veal is almost unknown, and veal chops are seldom broiled in the manner of steaks or lamb chops. Some cuts of beef are excellent roasted or broiled, but others require the gentler, moist-heat methods of braising or stewing.

Most parts of Europe are much farther removed than the Middle East from the practice of primitive fire-based cookery, but Western man has never quite lost the sense that there is something especially ceremonial (or symbolic of wealth) in cooking a large piece of meat by an open fire or the closest modern equivalent. The English are the great European practitioners of broiling and roasting; great hunks of fire-cooked beef have never lost the association of magnificence and lordliness that they possessed in simpler times. Plain steaks and roasts have always been glorified with something approaching spiritual fervor by British diners mistrustful of foreign fanciness. When Nathaniel Hawthorne remarked that the moral attitudes of Samuel Johnson the lexicographer were "as English an article as a beefsteak," he was appealing to a self-evident standard.

In Great Britain, as in America, animals are usually butchered so as to get the maximum number of sizable pieces for roasting and broiling. It was the English who began the first experiments in modern cattle-breeding, leading eventually to the development of specialized "beef types" like Angus, Hereford, and Shorthorn that were bred to provide ample amounts of steak and roasting meat. Strange to say, the steak-and-chop contingent that enjoyed the fruits of these developments while loudly decrying Frenchified sauces also enthusiastically supported another nineteenth-century novelty: the introduction of sharp-flavored bottled condiments seasoned with exotic ingredients (such as soy, tamarind, and chili peppers) from the distant reaches of the Anglo-Asian empire. Today many British and American diners would not dream of eating a broiled chop or steak without some bottled accompaniment such as Worcestershire sauce.

The English fondness for broiled foods has produced a specialty known as "mixed grill" ("grilling," which we reserve for broiling done with special pieces of equipment like grills or grill baskets, is the general British word for broiling). Traditionally, a mixed grill contains broiled lamb chops (or sometimes steak), tomatoes, sausages, mushrooms, lamb kidneys, bacon, and sometimes liver, all served up in one glorious presentation. Though it requires the organizational skills of a general to get everything separately broiled in time to be assembled on one table, the dish is too good not to be attempted at least once in a lifetime—and of course it is possible to serve an abridged version.

Throughout the Americas, some form of spit-barbecuing is known wherever ranching has been a way of life—Argentina, Paraguay and Uruguay, parts of Brazil and Mexico, and large areas of the southwestern United States. The very name "barbecue," and to some extent the technique, come to us from the American Indian. Early Spanish explorers described how food was dried and smoked in the West Indies on frameworks of sticks propped in front of fires. *Barbacoa* was their rendering of an Indian word for the stick platform. The Spanish then carried to other parts of the Americas a variant of the technique in which the meat was suspended over a fire of live coals or placed on an angled spit next to the open fire.

Today, Americans are great enthusiasts of every aspect of the art of broiling. In warm weather, the backyard barbecue all but replaces the kitchen stove; during the rest of the year, the oven broiler and electric grill are steadily in use. The variety of foods that are prepared this way seems inexhaustible and ranges from the ubiquitous but quite delicious hamburger to the elaborate extravaganza of suckling pig revolving slowly on a spit. It includes tender kebabs of beef, lamb, seafood, even vegetables; thick, juicy lamb chops to be cooked in minutes; succulent pork chops, toothsome spareribs; whole tenderloins of beef and every known variety of steak; entire legs of lamb, studded with rosemary and garlic; whole chickens rubbed with butter and roasted on a spit, or split into halves or cut into quarters, or quantities of chicken wings

and drumsticks to serve as finger food; tasty game birds and ducks cooked so the skin is crackling crisp; all sorts of fish for feasting while you watch your waistline; savory shrimps broiled in their shells; lobsters, split open, stuffed with herbs and bread crumbs; piquantly seasoned clams broiled to perfection or simply scrubbed and cooked over coals until they open of their own accord. The possibilities are limited only by your imagination.

At times, nothing can beat the ease and the simplicity of a broiled chicken or a chop—a perfect dinner for a busy, streamlined life. At other times, the relaxation and conviviality of cooking over fire out of doors make for splendidly casual summer parties.

Specialty stores now offer expensive packages of aromatic wood, such as mesquite from the Southwest, and bundles of exotic herbs, like fennel branches, to burn along with charcoal, thereby imparting special flavors to the food. The range of equipment for outdoor and indoor broiling is vast and growing steadily. But if your mind or pocketbook begins to ache when contemplating the purchase of a newer, better, bigger, more elaborate grill, you should remember that at base, the art of broiling is a very simple one. A quick hand and watchful eye will serve you better than a myriad of tools. And no equipment from a store can yet surpass the charm and pleasure of a campfire meal.

The lure of fire-based cookery has never faded for most of us. Whether it is charcoal-broiling, spit-roasting, hearth-cooking, communal barbecues, or the more modest expedient of panbroiling, there is something about the method that seems to bring out the flavors of certain foods in their simplest essence. Even now such approaches preserve some of the magic of primitive cookery, and even now they can restore the most jaded cook's faith in directness, simplicity, and the true flavor of good ingredients.

BROILING

Broiling or grilling is a dry-heat method suitable for tender meats and poultry and for many kinds of fish. The term "broiling" is used for cooking under a gas or electric broiler, whereas "grilling" is used for cooking over charcoal.

Pan-broiling (sometimes called "dry frying") is another dry heat method. Since no fat is used, the method is best for marbelized steaks or chops about 1 inch thick. A heavy iron skillet (preferably with ridges which give meat a quadrilled surface) is recommended.

Gas broilers produce an intense heat, which can be adjusted. The heat evaporates moisture as it is extracted from the food. Electric broilers are less hot; while it is easy to adjust the controls, the change takes longer to become effective. Since moisture can accumulate in electric broilers, it is necessary to leave the door slightly ajar to prevent steaming.

General Tips for Oven Broiling

The secret to success is to have the food cut to the right thickness and adjust the distance of the broiler rack from the heat source.
• For juicy interior and seared exterior, broil close to heat source for short time.
• For more even cooking, move the rack farther from the heat and cook for a longer time.
• Cook thicker pieces farther from heat source; cook thinner pieces quickly, and fairly close to heat source, for the longer a thin piece is exposed to heat, the more dried-out it will become.
• Let meats for broiling come to room temperature before you start. With frozen meats or poultry, be certain to defrost them completely.
• Do not season meats before broiling; salt tends to extract moisture and pepper can burn and become bitter.
• Arrange a drip pan under the rack to collect fats and juices extracted during cooking.
• The rack may be cold or hot; if it is preheated, there will be a pattern of the grill bars on the food. If grill is oiled, food will not stick. Or leave grill plain and oil meat well.
• Turn foods with tongs or 2 spoons; do not pierce them with a fork for that makes holes and causes loss of juices.
• Test for doneness by pressing with a finger; if meat is still uncooked, it will feel soft; if it is overdone, it will feel hard. If done just right, it should feel firm but still flexible.

Classic Marinade

Makes ½ cup

   freshly ground pepper
4 tablespoons olive oil
1 garlic clove, crushed
1 bay leaf
1 small sprig of fresh thyme, or ¼ teaspoon dried thyme
4 tablespoons lemon juice

Some variations: Add pinches of tarragon, rosemary or fresh parsley for marinating lamb, chicken or beef. Sage or savory for pork. Fresh dill for fish.

1 Use your hands to rub the surface of meat with freshly ground pepper. Use no salt.

2 Put oil, garlic and herbs into a large shallow bowl. Stir in lemon juice.

3 Add meat and turn over to coat well. Cover and leave in a cool place for 2 to 4 hours, turning occasionally to marinate evenly.

Broiling Meat

Various cuts of beef, pork and lamb are suitable. Veal is too delicate and too lacking in internal fat. Well-marbled cuts, such as steaks from prime beef, need no preparation, although they can be brushed with a thick coating of oil to prevent sticking.

Drier meats need to be brushed with oil or butter; or marinate them before broiling. Marinating is useful also for adding flavor variety to beef, lamb and pork.

When broiling steaks and chops, be sure to cut through the cartilage to prevent curling.

The following cuts of beef are recommended for broiling with one proviso applicable to all: *avoid overcooking.*

Rib Steak. 1 inch thick, weighing 1 to 1½ pounds, cook for a total of 15 minutes for rare, 20 minutes for medium.

Rib Eye Steak. (Also called Delmonico or fillet steak)—1 inch thick, weighing 8 to 10 ounces, cook for a total of 18 minutes for rare, 20 for medium.

Top Loin Steak. (Also called club steak, shell steak or strip steak)—1 inch thick, weighing 1 to 1½ pounds, cook for a total of 15 minutes for rare, 20 for medium.

T-bone Steak. 1 inch thick, weighing about 1½ pounds, cook for a total of 15 to 18 minutes for rare, 20 to 25 for medium.

Porterhouse Steak. 1 inch thick, weighing up to 2 pounds, cook for a total of 20 minutes for rare, 25 for medium.

Sirloin Steak. 1 inch thick, weighing about 3 pounds, cook for a total of 20 minutes for rare, 25 for medium.

Loin Top Sirloin. Boneless steak cut from the sirloin; cook like other sirloins.

Round Top Round Steak. (Often sold as London broil)—a prime or choice piece 1 inch thick, weighing 2 pounds, cook for a total of 20 minutes for rare, 25 for medium. Cut across the grain, making thin slices.

Tenderloin or Filet. The wide portion cut into 1-inch steaks can be broiled like a sirloin steak. The center of the filet can be cut into 2 chateaubriands, double-thick steaks, each ample for 2 servings.

The filet can be cut into little filets *(filets mignons),* 1 to 1½ inches thick, 6 to 8 ounces each, or into tournedos, about 1 inch thick, about 4 ounces each. Or *médaillons* can be cut from the tournedos slices. A filet mignon of 8 ounces should be cooked rare in 12 minutes, medium in 18 minutes. *Petits*

filets or kebabs can be cut from the narrowest end.

Flank Steak. (Often sold for London broil)—needs lengthy marinating to be tender, or should have the surface scored to break the long fibers. For a 1-inch-thick piece, weighing 2 pounds, cook for a total of 25 minutes for rare, 30 for medium. Cut across the grain at a diagonal, making thin slices.

Skirt Steak. For a piece 15 inches long and 4 inches wide, ½ inch thick, cook no more than 12 to 15

Broiling Beef Tournedos

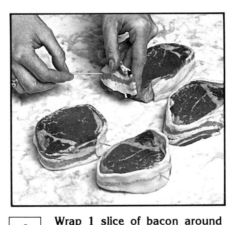

1 Wrap 1 slice of bacon around each steak. Secure with wooden toothpick. Heat broiler 20 minutes before serving time.

2 Place tournedos on broiler rack. Broil 3 inches from heat. 6 minutes per side for rare. 8 for medium. Do not serve well done.

3 Season cooked side according to taste. Using tongs, turn meat over. Broil, then season second side.

4 Tournedos can be garnished with broiled tomato halves (broil 5 inches from heat, 3 to 4 minutes) and maître d'hôtel butter.

minutes for rare, 15 to 18 for medium.

Ground Chuck or Top Round. —1-inch-thick patties, broil for 3 minutes per side for rare; 5 minutes per side for medium.

Broiling Pork

Since pork is young as it comes to market, the meat is tender. While we tend to think of pork as fatty meat, the fat is on the outside, and the grainy meat can dry out if not broiled with care. All pork should be cooked well, but not dried out.

Pork cuts that can be broiled successfully include shoulder blade steaks, loin back ribs (also called spareribs), all sorts of chops (rib, loin, sirloin, and smoked chops), tenderloin, ham steaks, and pork kebabs.

All pork for broiling needs to be brushed with oil, or marinated for 2 hours in advance. Basting during broiling will give moisture and juiciness and prevent drying of the outer portions.

Broil a blade steak ¾ inches thick for 20 to 25 minutes.

Chops 1 inch thick for 5 to 7 minutes on each side.

Tenderloin for 7 to 8 minutes on each side.

Ham steak (be sure to cut the edges to prevent curling) for 16 to 20 minutes.

Bacon must be watched carefully, and is best used to wrap other foods such as oysters, chicken livers, and beef tournedos.

Broiling Lamb

Lamb is excellent for broiling. It is young and tender when it comes to market, so it needs only gentle cooking. If your taste is for pink lamb, the time for broiling will be brief; for well-done lamb broil a little longer, but do not overcook it.

Portions of lamb that can be broiled include all kinds of chops—

Broiling Pork Chops

1 Marinated chops do not need brushing with oil. Use the marinade for brushing in step 4.

2 Turn the broiler to high and brush the grid with oil. Cook the chops close to heat for 1 to 2 minutes.

3 Turn chops, using tongs, and brown the other side. Reduce heat to low.

4 Continue cooking for another 5 to 7 minutes on each side, turning and brushing with the marinade.

5 Season the pork chops with salt and freshly ground black pepper. Garnish with parsley sprigs and serve immediately.

shoulder chops, rib chops, loin chops and sirloin chops.

Chops 1 inch thick will be cooked in 12 minutes total; sirloin chops may need an extra 2 minutes. If chops are thicker, add another 5 minutes total for each extra ½ inch of thickness.

Steaks cut from the leg are also good broiled; these are like sirloin chops, just larger around.

Kebabs, cut into 1½-inch cubes, need 12 to 18 minutes to be cooked. The exact time will be influenced by the other ingredients threaded on the skewers.

Noisettes (the tender piece of boneless meat cut from a lamb chop) should be cut about 1 inch thick. These can be barded with beef fat, fresh pork fat, or wrapped in bacon, then broiled like rib chops.

Butterflied leg of lamb—a small leg of lamb boned, opened out, and flattened as much as possible, requires care in cooking. A leg weighing 5 pounds after boning will need about 10 minutes per pound and will need to be turned often and well basted.

Broiling Chicken

Young tender birds, reaching market in 8 weeks, have a delicate taste, can be cooked quickly, and are adaptable to countless recipes and delicious accompaniments.

Chickens appropriate for broiling should weigh anywhere from 1½ to 2½ pounds. The chicken should be butterflied, split into halves, or quartered. Chicken parts are readily available and are ideal for broiling. Breasts have little fat and should be buttered and basted. All parts gain flavor and retain moisture if they are marinated and basted.

Wings and breasts cook faster than thighs and legs. Remove these as they are done, or cover these parts with foil if broiling whole or split birds.

Preparing for Broiling

If you have whole birds, split them or butterfly them. Cut off the wing tips as

Butterflying Chicken

1 Lay chicken on a board. Cut off oil sac and tail. Cut off any loose skin at the neck.

2 Cut through and along the breastbone to halve the bird. This bone is very soft so a sharp knife can easily do this.

3 Cut through the backbone with a sharp knife, or use poultry shears or kitchen scissors.

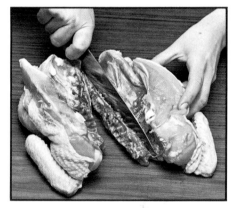

OR Remove backbone completely: cut along each side of it with a sharp knife and lift it out. Save for stock.

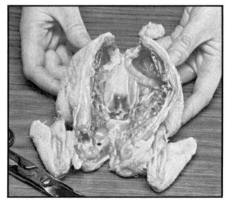

4 To butterfly a chicken, cut it into halves through the backbone and open it out flat, bone side down.

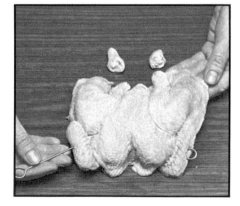

5 Run a sharp straight skewer through the leg and fleshy part of wing on each side, to hold bird flat during broiling.

Filleting, Boning and Skinning Fish

1 To scale, hold fish by tail and use blunt side of knife to scrape scales off towards the head.

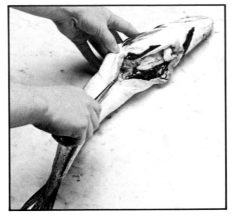

2 To gut fish, make a slit along the belly from below the gills along two thirds of the body length.

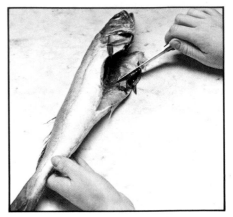

3 Scrape out inside of belly. Rub cavity with salt and scrape away black skin inside cavity.

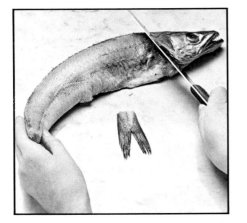

5 To remove the tail, cut through the fish at its thinnest part. Cut off the head just behind the gills.

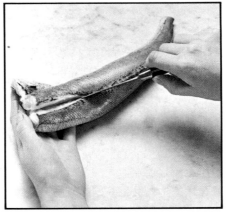

6 To fillet, cut along the backbone down to the tail end. Cut into the flesh, not just through the skin.

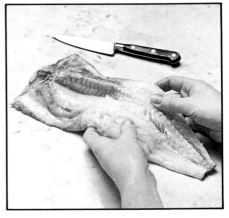

7 Cut the fish from belly cavity to tail and open it out flat by easing the belly cavity open.

9 To skin a fresh fillet work a knife between the skin and flesh at tail end. Work skin away by hand.

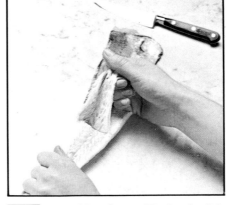

10 To skin a frozen fillet lay the fish flesh side down and pull off skin from tail end.

11 To bone, press the fish, belly side down, along its backbone to open slightly without halving it.

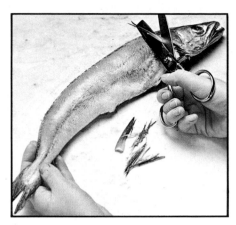

4 Cut off the gill covers (the little fins behind the head) on both sides of the fish.

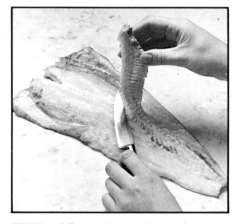

8 Lift out the backbone from the head end. Ease the flesh from the backbone. Cut fillets into halves.

12 Cut through the bone at head end and ease away the backbone. Cut through at tail end and lift clear.

they can easily burn. Open wing joint so it will lie flat; open thigh joint also. If not severed, the tendons in these parts shrink in broiling and cause leg and wing ends to stick up and they can easily burn.

Chicken pieces may be seasoned, but a better idea is to season between skin and flesh. Pull skin gently away from flesh and insert flavored butter and seasoning. Use your fingers. Brush outsides with oil and/or butter, or use a barbecue sauce, or marinate and baste with remaining marinade.

Start cooking with bone side toward the heat. After 5 minutes turn with tongs. Cook for 5 to 8 minutes on the skin side. Turn twice more, cooking for a total of 20 to 30 minutes, according to thickness of pieces. Turn often so outer portions do not dry out, and baste with each turn.

Other Poultry

Pieces of fatty birds—duck, goose, capon—can be broiled successfully and need less care in basting and marinating; whole capons, ducks and geese should be cooked by other methods. Turkey parts, because of their thickness, are better cooked by other methods. Small birds—squabs, Cornish game hens, game birds—can be split and broiled like small chicken broilers. However, they all lack natural fat and require basting.

Broiling Fish

Fish is naturally tender and quick to cook by most methods. Broiling is especially good for fatty fish, but it is hard to be certain which species are fat and which are lean since the texture varies according to their diet and the season when they are caught. However, we can count as fatty fish bluefish, herring, mackerel, mullet, salmon, shad, smelts and tuna. Lean fish that can be broiled include cod, haddock and hake; flounders, halibut and sole; black seabass; largemouth and smallmouth bass; striped bass; sea robin; and monkfish. Swordfish and stur-

geon, which are rather dry-textured, are also good broiled if the slices are thick enough. Very soft-textured fish such as whiting tend to fall apart in broiling; this can also happen with bluefish, so when broiling fillets do not turn them.

To broil lean or dry fish, rinse and pat dry. Heat broiler. Place fish on oiled cold grill over a shallow pan, or in a broiler pan with a rack. Do one of the following:
• Brush fish with melted butter and/or oil.
• Spread fish with a savory topping (flavored bread crumbs dotted with butter, egg and crumbs, mayonnaise, sauce).
• Marinate fish before cooking and baste with marinade during broiling.

Thick fish that needs extra minutes also needs extra basting. Broil fish under moderate heat. When first side is done, turn; steaks can be turned with a pancake turner or wide spatula; fillets thick enough to be turned may need 2 spatulas to be turned without breaking. Average fillets are thin and need no turning.

When fish is ready, it will flake at once when tested with a fork. If fish has bones, flesh should come cleanly away from the bones. Do not overcook fish.

Broil fillets for 3 to 5 minutes on each side, 5 minutes total for fillets that are not turned.

If the fillet has skin on one side, broil it skin side toward heat source for 2 minutes, then reduce heat to moderate and turn skin side down. On an electric stove, keep heat moderate but broil skin side very close to heat source, then return rack to the usual level, 4 to 5 inches from heat source.

Broil steaks for 6 to 12 minutes per side according to thickness.

Broil whole fish for 5 to 15 minutes per side according to thickness of the fish.

Treat defrosted frozen fish in the same way, but use a little more butter or oil. Frozen fish can be broiled from the frozen state if the pieces are thin enough. Just allow a little extra time to be sure pieces are done to the center of the thickest part.

Cutting Chicken Parts

1 To make chicken quarters, first cut chicken into halves. Lay halves skin side up and cut diagonally between leg and wing.

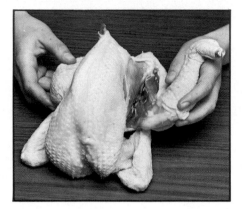

2 To joint a chicken, first cut leg away from body. Pull the leg toward you so the joint is exposed.

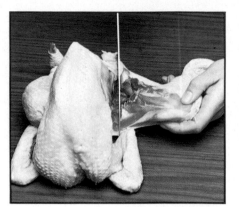

3 Cut through the moist pink part of this ball-and-socket joint. Cut off the other leg.

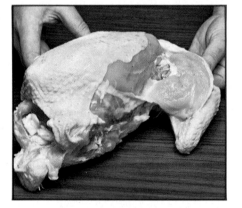

4 To remove the wing, slice into the breast meat to make a better portion. Pull wing away to expose the joint.

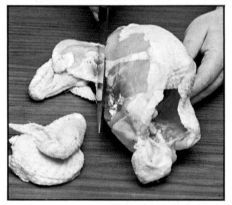

5 Then cut through the joint to sever the wing. Fold it into a neat package with the attached breast meat underneath.

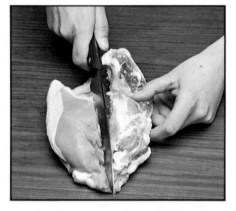

6 To remove the whole breast, cut through the rib bones along the side of the body to separate breast from the back.

7 Cut down the center of the breastbone to divide breast into 2 portions. Large breasts may be split again to make 4 portions.

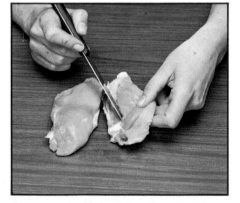

8 Pull skin away gently for skinless breasts. For boneless pieces, insert knife between rib bones and flesh: cut away bones.

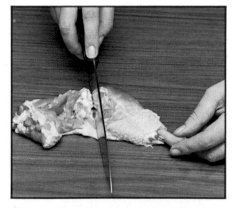

9 Divide large legs into thighs and drumsticks by cutting through the center ball-and-socket joint.

Fatty fish are cooked in the same fashion as lean or dry fish. The preparations for broiling are also the same, and the timing as well. However, do not suppose that because these are labeled "fatty" that they need no care in the broiler. The grill should be oiled, and the outside portions of the fish should be very lightly brushed with oil to prevent sticking to the grill. Some fatty fish are marinated; in that case baste with the marinade during broiling. If you are cooking whole fish, cut a few diagonal slits along each side, to help heat to penetrate to the interior and to prevent curling from contraction of the flesh. Avoid overcooking.

Fish roes can also be broiled. These need to be treated like dry fish, well buttered or covered with a coating. Do not put them on the grill, but use a flat pan or baking dish. Plan to turn them only once since they are very fragile.

Flavoring Broiled Foods

Aside from specific marinades, another versatile way to add flavor to broiled foods is with the use of compound butters. The butters can be stored in the refrigerator for a week.

Those containing only herbs can be frozen and will keep 3 months.

Compound Butters

Since these butters keep so well, it is practical to prepare at least 8 ounces at a time. While a compound butter can be served hot, like a butter sauce, it is more usual to serve a slice of the cold butter on hot food, where it will slowly melt and release the delicious flavor. This amount will give you about 20 slices.

The photos show the procedure for making this butter, but the same

Compound Butters

Maître d' Hôtel Butter

8 ounces unsalted butter
6 tablespoons minced fresh parsley
4 teaspoons fresh lemon juice
salt and pepper

1 Cut butter into rough pieces, place in a bowl, and let it come to room temperature.

2 Add minced parsley and beat with softened butter until butter is smooth and creamy and evenly flecked with green.

3 Add lemon juice and seasonings to taste. Beat until there are no droplets of lemon juice on the surface of the butter.

4 Wet hands with cold water and roll the butter into a smooth oval, then into an even roll. Pat ends into shape.

5 Wrap the roll in greaseproof paper and refrigerate for 3 hours, or until firm.

method is used for others. For another flavor, omit parsley and lemon juice and substitute the ingredients listed. A food processor can be used to chop or mince the various ingredients, but they should be mixed with the butter by hand to avoid overprocessing.

• *Anise butter:* 3 tablespoons Pernod, Pastis or Ricard. Excellent with fish.

• *Blue cheese butter:* 4 ounces blue cheese, crumbled and softened.

• *Chive butter:* 2 tablespoons snipped fresh chives.

• *Coriander butter:* 4 teaspoons ground coriander plus a little grated orange rind.

• *Curry butter:* 1½ to 2 tablespoons curry powder; sauté curry powder in a little butter before adding it to the rest.

• *Garlic butter:* 4 garlic cloves, peeled and put through a press, 4 teaspoons minced fresh parsley, 1 tablespoon lemon juice.

• *Green herb butter:* 6 tablespoons mixed minced herbs (parsley, chives, tarragon, chervil) and 4 teaspoons lemon juice. Good for steaks, chops and fish.

• *Mint butter:* 2 tablespoons minced fresh mint.

• *Mustard butter:* 4 tablespoons prepared Dijon-style mustard and 2 tablespoons minced fresh parsley. Good for steaks, chops, liver, fish.

• *Mustard-watercress butter:* Add 4 tablespoons minced watercress leaves to a mustard butter.

• *Rosemary butter:* 4 teaspoons minced fresh rosemary.

• *Shrimp butter:* 6 ounces peeled cooked shrimps, 1½ tablespoons fresh lemon juice and ½ teaspoon salt, ground in a blender or food processor until smooth.

• *Snail butter:* 4 tablespoons minced shallots, 2 garlic cloves, peeled and put through a press, and 2 tablespoons minced fresh parsley. Good for meat or

fish; it is served with snails, which gives it the name.

• *Tarragon butter:* 3 tablespoons minced fresh tarragon, or 3 teaspoons crumbled dried tarragon, and 4 tablespoons fresh lemon juice.

• *Shellfish butter:* This is more complicated. 8 ounces cooked whole shrimps in shells or 1 pound cooked shellfish parts such as legs and shells; 2 teaspoons fresh lemon juice, 1 teaspoon salt and ½ teaspoon white pepper. Chop shrimps or shellfish parts. Melt butter. Process half of shellfish and half of butter at a time in a blender or food processor to a smooth paste. Place mixture in a saucepan over low heat and let it barely simmer for 12 minutes. Pour through a strainer into a clean pan, then pour a little boiling water through the shell mixture again to get every bit of flavor. Now strain the butter again, this time though a sieve lined with a double layer of moistened cheesecloth. Add lemon juice and salt and pepper. Beat to mix well. This butter adds color and flavor to sauces for fish and shellfish.

Loin Chops with Sauce Robert

4 portions

4	center-cut loin pork chops
2	tablespoons oil

Demi-glace sauce

1	small carrot
1	celery rib
1	small onion
⅓	cup mushroom stems
4	bacon slices
3	tablespoons butter
2½	tablespoons flour
2½	cups good brown stock
1	bouquet garni
2	teaspoons tomato purée
½	cup jellied brown stock

Sauce Robert

1	small onion
2	tablespoons butter
½	cup white wine
3	small gherkins
4	teaspoons Dijon mustard
1	teaspoon chopped parsley
	salt
	freshly ground pepper

This dish is a study in contrasts; a long-simmered brown sauce is used with chops that are broiled in minutes. Demi-glace, one of the base, or "mother" sauces of French cuisine, is

here transformed into a sauce Robert, piquant with wine, gherkins, and Dijon mustard.

• You can prepare the demi-glace sauce ahead of time (through step 9) and make extra by doubling the ingredients. Keep refrigerated up to several days, or freeze in small containers.

• A classic demi-glace simmers for 8 hours or longer. For this streamlined version, be sure to simmer sauce for the times indicated, for full-flavored results.

• This sauce can be used equally well with steak or lamb chops.

• Try to find the small French gherkins called *cornichons*, available in the gourmet department of supermarkets and in specialty shops.

Loin Chops with Sauce Robert (continued)

 Wash carrot and celery, peel onion, chop with mushrooms. Remove bacon rind and chop bacon.

2 Melt butter in a medium-size heavy pan. Add the bacon, cover pan and cook over low heat for 2 minutes.

3 Add the vegetables and cook over low heat until onion softens. Stir occasionally.

 Add a spoonful of cold stock or water. Let the fat rise to surface and skim off. Do this again. Add tomato purée.

8 Strain sauce through a sieve, into a small saucepan, pressing all juices from the vegetables.

 Add the jellied stock. Simmer until the demi-glace sauce has reduced to 1½ cups, about 30 minutes.

 Add the wine and simmer to reduce by half. Add to demi-glace; simmer for 20 minutes.

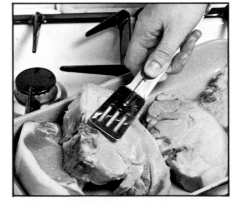

 Broil chops for 1 minute on each side. Reduce heat or lower dish and broil for 5 to 7 minutes on each side, basting.

15 Chop gherkins. When sauce is ready, stir in mustard, gherkins and parsley. Season to taste. Do not reheat.

4 Add flour and cook, stirring constantly, until the roux is a rich nut brown. Heat 2½ cups of stock in another saucepan.

5 Remove from the heat and gradually add the warm stock, whisking continuously. Bring to a boil.

6 Add the bouquet garni, cover and simmer for 1 to 2 hours. Skim off any fat that rises with a skimming spoon.

10 Brush the loin chops on both sides with a little of the oil. Set aside until ready to cook.

11 Turn broiler to highest heat and arrange the chops in single layer in gratin dish.

12 Continue the sauce. Peel and chop onion. Melt butter in small heavy pan; cook onion till soft.

16 Place pork chops on warmed serving dish. Spoon a little sauce over and around each portion of meat.

Smoked Pork Chops with Mustard

4 portions

4 smoked pork loin chops
  olive oil
2 ounces butter, softened

4 teaspoons grainy mustard
  or Dijon-style mustard

Snip the edges of the chops at intervals to prevent curling during broiling. Brush broiler pan with oil, then heat broiler, pan and rack to medium. Mix the softened butter with the mustard until homogeneous, then spread the mustard butter over both sides of the chops.

Place chops on the rack and broil for about 5 minutes on each side, depending on thickness, and baste with the juices from the pan several times. Serve at once.

Variations: For herb chops, omit mustard and mix butter with 2 teaspoons dried sage. For chili chops, omit the mustard and mix the butter with a little chili sauce to taste.

Country-Style Pork Chops

4 portions

1 small onion
2 juicy oranges
1 tablespoon olive oil
  black pepper

1 sprig of fresh rosemary, or
  1 teaspoon dried
  rosemary
4 pork loin or shoulder
  chops

Peel the onion and mince it. Grate the rind of both oranges and squeeze the juice from one of them. Put onion, orange rind and juice, the olive oil, a good grinding of black pepper, and the rosemary in a glass or pottery dish. Mix with a fork. Put the chops in the mixture and turn to coat both sides. Cover the dish with foil and let chops marinate in the refrigerator for 2 to 8 hours.

Preheat broiler. Remove chops from the dish, drain briefly, then broil under high heat for 1 minute on each side, to sear the surface. Lower the broiler pan and broil for about 7 minutes longer on each side, brushing occasionally with the marinade. Meanwhile, peel remaining orange and cut into 4 thick slices. Cover each chop with an orange slice and brush oranges with the marinade. Broil for 4 minutes longer, until orange slices are hot and chops completely cooked.

Filet Mignon with Blue Cheese

4 portions

4 tablespoons blue cheese,
    at room temperature
2 tablespoons unsalted
    butter, at room
    temperature
1 tablespoon minced shallot

1 teaspoon Angostura bitters
4 filets mignons, each 1½
    inches thick
    olive oil
    salt and pepper

Preheat broiler. Combine cheese, butter, shallot and bitters; cream to a smooth paste. Set aside. Brush steaks with oil and place on the broiler rack. Broil 3 inches from the heat source for about 1 minute on each side, to seal the surface. Lower the broiler pan to 5 inches from the heat source and broil for another 3 minutes on each side for rare, 5 minutes on each

side for medium rare or longer according to taste. Remove steaks from broiler and season with salt and pepper.

Transfer steaks to a heated platter or individual plates and top each one with a generous mound of the topping. Serve at once, before the topping melts.

Chateaubriand with Duchesse Potatoes

4 portions

2 **chateaubriand steaks, each about 12 ounces** olive oil	8 **ounces mushroom caps** 4 **medium-size tomatoes** salt and black pepper watercress bouquets

Duchesse Potatoes

1 **pound potatoes** 1 **ounce butter** 2 **tablespoons milk, hot**	1 **large egg, lightly beaten** salt and white pepper

Preheat oven to 425°F. Peel potatoes and simmer until tender, about 20 minutes. Drain potatoes and mix in the butter until melted, then the hot milk, beaten egg, and salt and white pepper to taste. Mash the potatoes thoroughly, or purée in a food processor. Spoon potatoes into a large piping bag. With a no. 8 star tip, pipe out mounds of potatoes on a baking sheet. Brown them in the oven for 30 minutes.

Meanwhile, preheat the broiler. Brush the steaks with olive oil and broil them close to the heat source for about 1 minute on each side, to seal the surface. Lower the broiling pan and continue to broil, turning each steak to cook evenly on both sides. Broil for 12 to 14 minutes for rare; 14 to 16 minutes for medium; 16 to 18 minutes for well done.

While potatoes and steaks are cooking, wipe mushroom caps with a damp cloth. Cut away the peel on top to decorate them like minarets. Wash tomatoes, halve them crosswise, brush with olive oil, and sprinkle with salt and pepper. Add mushrooms and tomato halves to the broiler pan for the last 5 minutes that the steak is being cooked. Season the steaks with salt and pepper and transfer to a warmed serving platter. With a spatula, transfer potato mounds, tomatoes and mushrooms to the platter. Add watercress bouquets and serve at once. Each Chateaubriand will make 2 portions.

Variation: Put the steaks, almost done, on a plank and surround with mushrooms and tomatoes. Pipe duchesse potatoes in a ring around steak and vegetables and finish in the broiler, until steak is done and potatoes browned. Put a knob of savory butter on top of each steak.

Bistecca alla Fiorentina
(Marinated Steak, Florentine Style)

4 portions

1 porterhouse, sirloin or T-bone steak, 2 pounds, 1 inch thick
3 tablespoons olive oil
3 tablespoons red-wine vinegar
2 garlic cloves, put through a press

1 bay leaf
1 teaspoon crumbled dried thyme
1 teaspoon crumbled dried orégano
2 tablespoons chopped parsley
¾ cup dry red wine
salt and pepper

Place steak in a shallow glass or pottery dish. Combine remaining ingredients except salt and pepper. Pour marinade over the steak, cover, and let it stand at room temperature for 5 hours, or refrigerate for 8 hours. Turn steak and baste from time to time.

Preheat broiler. Remove steak from marinade and pat dry. Reserve marinade. Broil steak 3 to 4 inches from the heat source for 4 minutes on each side for rare, or longer according to taste. Transfer to a heated serving dish.

Combine marinade with pan juices in a small saucepan. Reduce over high heat to half its volume. Season steak with salt and pepper. Serve the sauce separately.

Entrecôtes à la Bretonne

4 portions

4 beef rib steaks (entrecôtes)
olive oil
3 shallots or 1 small onion
½ garlic clove

3 ounces butter
2 teaspoons lemon juice
2 tablespoons chopped fresh parsley
salt and black pepper

Brush the steaks with a little oil. Preheat the broiler. Peel and mince the shallots and garlic. Melt 1 ounce of the butter over low heat and cook shallots and garlic in the butter until they are very soft and tender. Add remaining butter, lemon juice and parsley. When butter is all melted, keep the sauce warm over hot water.

Broil the steaks under high heat for about 1 minute on each side to seal the surface. Lower the broiler pan and cook the steaks for 2½ to 5 minutes on each side, until done to your taste. Season steaks with salt and pepper and turn them in the butter sauce until both sides are buttered. Serve at once. For Breton vegetables, serve button mushrooms with tiny onions and tiny green snap beans, cooked whole.

Butterflied Leg of Lamb with Vodka Sauce

8 portions

1 leg of lamb, 6 pounds
5 garlic cloves

2 cups French dressing
2 cups seasoned dry bread crumbs

Vodka Sauce

2 cups tomato ketchup
¼ cup cider vinegar
½ teaspoon liquid smoke

3 tablespoons brown sugar
¼ teaspoon black pepper
¼ cup (2 ounces) vodka

Have the butcher bone and butterfly the leg of lamb. With a sharp-pointed knife make incisions in the surface of the meat and the fatty exterior. Peel all the garlic cloves; set two aside for the sauce, and cut the others into slivers. Insert a garlic sliver into each incision in the lamb. Rub French dressing all over the lamb and let it marinate, covered, for 4 to 6 hours, or overnight in the refrigerator.

Preheat broiler. Remove lamb from marinade and place on the broiler rack. Broil 5 inches from the heat source for 5 minutes, then sprinkle the surface with some of the bread crumbs. Broil for 5 minutes longer, then turn lamb over and broil on the second side for 5 minutes. Sprinkle second side with some bread crumbs and continue. Keep turning the lamb and sprinkling with more bread crumbs until the crust is crisp and brown and the lamb done to your taste, 25 to 30 minutes for pink lamb.

Meanwhile, combine ketchup, vinegar, liquid smoke, brown sugar and pepper. Put remaining 2 garlic cloves through a press into the mixture. Bring to a boil, stirring, then simmer for 10 minutes. Stir in vodka and simmer for 1 minute. Pour sauce into warmed sauceboat and keep warm. Carve the lamb and serve with the vodka sauce.

Rack of Lamb with Tomatoes

6 portions

2 racks of lamb, each with 6 chops
3 ounces butter

6 large tomatoes
salt and pepper

Have the chine bones removed from the racks and the bones cracked at the joints. Cut down between the ends of the chop bones about 2 inches and remove the meat. (This lamb can be used for stock.) Trim the bones completely. Lay the meat fat side up and make diagonal cuts across the fat. Make cuts in the opposite direction to make a diamond pattern. Preheat the broiler. Rub the lamb with 1 ounce of the butter. Place the racks bone side up on the broiler pan and broil for 5 minutes. Turn fat side up and broil for 5 minutes. Lower the pan and broil on the bone side for 15 minutes, basting with the pan drippings occasionally. Turn fat side up and broil until the fat is crisp and brown and the lamb done to taste, about 10 minutes longer. If you prefer lamb well done, broil a few minutes longer on each side.

While lamb is being cooked, prepare tomatoes. Cut them crosswise into halves. Melt remaining butter and brush cut sides of the tomatoes. Add to the lamb racks to broil for about 5 minutes. Season tomatoes with salt and pepper. Place racks on a warmed serving platter, fat side up, and surround with the tomatoes. Put a chop frill on each bone.

To carve the racks, cut down between the chop bones. Hold the end of the chop by the paper frill and gently separate from the rack. Serve 2 chops and 2 tomato halves for each portion.

Lamb Chops with Mint, Turkish Style

4 portions

1 small cucumber
½ small onion
½ to ¾ cup natural yogurt
2 teaspoons minced fresh mint leaves

salt and pepper
8 rib lamb chops
olive oil
2 bunches of fresh mint sprigs

Peel the cucumber, halve it lengthwise, and scoop out any seeds. Mince the cucumber and put the pieces into a bowl. Peel and grate the onion and add to cucumber. Stir in yogurt, minced mint, and salt and pepper to taste. Mix well. Put the sauce into a serving bowl and keep it cool.

Trim the ends of the chop bones. Preheat broiler, with broiler pan and rack in position. Brush chops with oil on both sides, then broil under high heat for 1 minute on each side, to sear the surface. Lower the broiler pan and cook chops for 3 to 5 minutes on each side, until done to your taste. Put a paper chop frill on each bone, and arrange chops on a bed of mint sprigs. Serve at once, with the sauce as accompaniment.

Tandoori-Style Chicken

4 portions

1½ ounces fresh gingerroot
2 garlic cloves
1 teaspoon sesame seeds
1 teaspoon coriander seeds
1 teaspoon cumin seeds
1 cup natural yogurt
2 tablespoons tomato purée
    or ½ teaspoon red food
    coloring

1 large broiler-fryer, 3½
    pounds, or 4 chicken
    quarters
salt and pepper
4 teaspoons lemon juice
2 tablespoons butter
   fresh coriander leaves
2 lemons

Peel gingerroot and garlic and chop into very small pieces. In a mortar or a spice grinder, crush sesame, coriander and cumin seeds. Mix all these ingredients into the yogurt, add tomato purée, and mix well. Halve and quarter the whole chicken, cutting along the backbone and removing it. Remove fat and skin from chicken pieces and make 3 or 4 incisions in each piece. Place chicken in a glass or pottery dish and spoon marinade over. Cover and leave for 8 hours, turning the pieces over occasionally.

Preheat broiler to medium. Remove chicken from marinade and season with salt and pepper. Place chicken pieces, bone side up, in the broiler pan without the rack. Pour lemon juice over the pieces and dot with butter. Broil 5 inches from the heat source for 12 minutes, basting 2 or 3 times. Turn pieces over, baste with the pan juices, and broil for 8 minutes longer, again basting 2 or 3 times. Test with a skewer to see that meat is cooked to your taste. Place chicken on a warmed serving dish and garnish with coriander leaves and the lemons, cut into wedges.

Variation: Use watercress or parsley if you have no fresh coriander.

Broiled Chicken with Lemon Marinade

4 portions

4	chicken pieces	4	watercress sprigs
1	lemon		

Lemon Marinade

1	garlic clove	3	tablespoons olive oil
1	teaspoon salt	3	tablespoons lemon juice
½	teaspoon black pepper	1	bay leaf

Make the marinade: Peel and slice garlic and crush with the salt under a knife blade. Put in a glass or pottery dish and add pepper, oil, lemon juice and bay leaf. Stir well. Put chicken pieces in the marinade, turn to coat both sides, and cover. Leave in a cool place for at least 2 hours.

Preheat broiler to medium. Place chicken, bone side up, in the broiler pan and broil 5 inches from the heat source for 15 minutes, basting frequently with remaining marinade. Turn chicken skin side up and broil for 10 minutes longer, basting frequently with marinade. Test with a skewer; juices should be clear and skin crisp. Serve on a hot dish, with lemon quarters and watercress sprigs.

Country-Style Chicken

4 portions

1	broiler-fryer, about 3 pounds	4	thick slices of bacon
1	large lemon	8	ounces button mushrooms
3	ounces butter	4	pickled crabapples or peaches

Halve the chicken by cutting along the breastbone, then cutting along the backbone and removing backbone. Cut each half into 2 pieces. Run a small skewer through leg or wing to the opposite side to keep the piece as flat as possible. Cut the lemon and rub the cut sides over the chicken, squeezing juice over the pieces. Melt butter and brush all over chicken on both sides. Preheat broiler to medium.

Arrange chicken pieces, bone side up, on the broiler pan and broil 5 inches below the heat source for 12 to 15 minutes. Meanwhile, halve the bacon slices and roll them into a curl, fastening with a food pick. Trim mushrooms, wipe with a damp cloth, and brush with some of remaining butter.

Turn chicken skin side up, brush with remaining butter or pan juices, and continue to broil for 5 minutes. Arrange bacon and mushrooms in the pan and continue to broil chicken and bacon until both are done to your taste, basting with pan juices now and then. When chicken skin is crisp and bacon and mushrooms cooked, transfer all to a warmed serving dish and garnish with crabapples or peaches.

Variations: For almond chicken, omit bacon and mushrooms and garnish with 3 ounces slivered almonds, sautéed in butter until golden and mixed with a little lemon juice. For pineapple chicken, omit bacon and mushrooms. Brush 4 pineapple rings with butter and broil until golden. Broil 4 chipolata sausages at the same time and thread each one through the pineapple ring. Arrange on top of the chicken pieces.

Broiled Chicken Dijonnaise

4 portions

1 broiler-fryer chicken, about 3 pounds	¼ teaspoon dried tarragon
3 ounces unsalted butter	2 teaspoons Worcestershire sauce
2 garlic cloves	1 teaspoon fresh lemon juice
4 tablespoons Dijon-style mustard	salt and pepper
	1 cup fresh white bread crumbs

Preheat broiler. Cut chicken into halves or quarters. Melt the butter. Brush chicken pieces on both sides with melted butter. Place pieces on the broiler pan with skin side down. Broil 5 inches from the heat source for about 10 minutes on each side, until chicken is lightly browned. Baste with some of the melted butter every 5 minutes.

While chicken is broiling, peel garlic and push through a press into a small bowl. Add mustard, tarragon, Worcestershire sauce, lemon juice, and salt and pepper to taste. Mix well.

Remove broiler pan and pour off all the juices into a cup. Let fat rise to the surface, then remove it with a spoon or paper towels. Whisk enough of the juices into the mustard mixture, drop by drop, to thicken it to the consistency of a mayonnaise. Gently stir in bread crumbs. Spread mixture over chicken on the skin side, and broil again for about 5 minutes, until the topping is golden brown. Transfer to a heated platter and serve at once.

Deviled Chicken

4 portions

1 broiler-fryer, about 3 pounds	2 teaspoons superfine granulated sugar
2½ ounces butter	½ teaspoon salt
1 teaspoon dry mustard	½ teaspoon paprika
2 teaspoons curry powder	1 teaspoon Worcestershire sauce
	3 slices of 2-day-old bread

Quarter the chicken; remove the backbone. Skewer each piece so that it will lie flat. Melt butter in a small saucepan and stir in mustard, curry powder, sugar, salt, paprika and Worcestershire sauce. Keep the devil sauce over low heat. Preheat broiler to medium and oven to 350°F.

Brush chicken pieces on both sides with half of the sauce. Arrange pieces bone side up in a shallow flameproof dish. Broil 5 inches from the heat source for 5 minutes, then turn and broil for 5 minutes on the skin side. Meanwhile remove crusts from bread and grate the bread, or process in a food processor, to make fine crumbs. Reheat the devil sauce, stir in the crumbs, and remove from heat. Spoon the moistened crumbs evenly over the top of the chicken.

Transfer the dish to the oven and bake the chicken for 30 minutes. Serve the dish hot or cold.

Chicken in Spicy Tomato Sauce

4 portions

4 chicken portions	4 green pepper rings
2 ounces butter	

Spicy Tomato Sauce

1 small onion	2 teaspoons brown sugar
4 tablespoons tomato purée	1 teaspoon dry mustard
2 tablespoons water	½ teaspoon salt
2 tablespoons red-wine vinegar	

Make the sauce: Grate the onion into a bowl. Add all other sauce ingredients and stir until sugar and mustard are dissolved. Preheat broiler to medium. Melt the butter in a small saucepan and brush a little of it over the chicken. Arrange chicken pieces in the broiler pan without the rack and bone side up, and broil 5 inches from the heat source for 5 minutes. Turn pieces over and broil for another 5 minutes.

Spoon the sauce into the saucepan with remaining melted butter and simmer for 5 minutes. Brush the chicken with sauce and continue to broil, brushing with sauce every 5 minutes. Chicken will be fully cooked in 30 minutes. Transfer chicken to a serving dish, spoon any remaining sauce over, and garnish each piece with a pepper ring.

Broiled Striped Bass with Fennel

6 portions

1 striped bass, 6 to 8 pounds, whole—dressed and scaled	2 tablespoons fresh lemon juice
3 dozen dried fennel stalks	1 tablespoon chopped parsley
2 ounces unsalted butter, softened	salt and pepper
	olive oil
	1 ounce brandy

Preheat broiler. Pat fish dry and score each side with 3 or 4 slashes along the body. Insert a fennel stalk in each incision and about 6 stalks inside the fish. Combine butter, lemon juice, parsley, and salt and pepper to taste. Spread a little of the butter mixture into each incision in the fish. Brush the fish with oil. Set the fish on the broiler rack and broil 6 inches from the heat source for about 6 minutes. Carefully turn fish over, brush again with oil, and broil for 5 to 10 minutes longer, until fish tests done.

Arrange the rest of the fennel stalks on a large flameproof serving dish, and place the rack of fish on top. Heat the brandy in a large metal spoon or a small saucepan; ignite brandy and pour over fish. Fennel stalks will ignite and the smoke will flavor the bass. Let fish stand over the fennel for 10 minutes before serving.

Broiled Split Mackerel

4 portions

4 fresh mackerels, each about 12 ounces	1 pound fresh gooseberries
salt and pepper	6 ounces salted butter
corn oil	grated nutmeg

Have fishmonger dress the mackerels: remove heads, viscera and gill covers. Cut the mackerels open along the ventral side, leaving them attached along the back. Press the backbone to make the fish lie flat. Sprinkle the open side of the fishes with salt and pepper and brush with a little corn oil. Let mackerels reach room temperature.

Top and tail the gooseberries, wash them, and put them in a saucepan with 2 cups water and a little salt. Simmer for 10 minutes. Pour off the water and stir in the butter, a little black pepper and nutmeg to taste. Simmer the sauce until berries are very soft. Put the sauce through a sieve to remove the seeds. Return sauce to low heat and keep hot.

Preheat broiler and oil broiler rack. Broil the mackerels first on the opened side 5 inches from the heat source for 6 to 8 minutes. Turn over and broil on the skin side for 6 minutes longer. Serve the fish with the warm sauce. The tart gooseberry taste is excellent with the somewhat fatty mackerel.

Salmon Steaks Florentine

4 portions

2 pounds fresh spinach	juice of ½ lemon
4 salmon steaks (chinook or atlantic), each about 1 inch thick	4 lemon slices salt and white pepper cayenne pepper
6 ounces unsalted butter	¼ cup heavy cream

Remove stems from spinach and discard any damaged leaves. Wash spinach thoroughly in several waters, and drain well. Pack it in a large saucepan with only the water that clings to the leaves and cover. Cook over high heat until spinach starts to sizzle. Turn it over with a wooden spoon and continue cooking for 8 to 10 minutes, turning as needed. Spinach should be cooked but not discolored. Turn spinach into a colander and press to extract moisture. Chop in the colander to small pieces and leave to drain further.

Preheat broiler to medium. Dot salmon steaks with 2 ounces of the butter and broil for 6 to 8 minutes. Use a wide spatula to turn steaks over and broil for 6 minutes longer, basting with pan juices now and then.

Melt remaining butter in a saucepan and add lemon juice and seasoning to taste. Keep butter sauce warm. Return chopped spinach to the saucepan, pour in the cream, and heat to very hot. Spoon spinach on a deep serving dish and arrange the salmon steaks on top. Pour butter sauce over the salmon, decorate with lemon twists and serve at once.

Broiled Swordfish

4 portions

2 swordfish steaks, 1 to 1½ inches thick, each 12 to 14 ounces
4 tablespoons olive oil
juice of 1 lemon

2 tablespoons minced parsley
2 garlic cloves
salt and pepper
4 teaspoons vinegar-packed capers, drained

Wipe swordfish steaks with a damp cloth and cut each into 2 portions. Mix oil, lemon juice and parsley. Peel garlic and put through a press into the oil. Add seasoning to taste. Mix well. Preheat broiler.

Brush swordfish with some of the oil mixture and place on the broiler pan. Broil 5 inches from the heat source for about 7 minutes. Use a broad spatula to turn the steaks over, brush with more of the oil mixture, and broil for about 5 minutes longer. Fish should be cooked but not dried out. Combine the pan juices with any remaining oil mixture and the capers and spoon the mixture equally over the portions.

Broiled Scallops

4 portions

1¼ pounds sea scallops
4 ounces butter
juice of 1 lemon
1 teaspoon paprika

salt and pepper
1 cup soft fresh bread crumbs
lemon wedges

If sea scallops are very large, halve them. Place them into a colander or large strainer and quickly rinse them with a hose or pour cold water over them. Do not let them soak. Let scallops drain, then roll in paper towels to dry. Melt the butter and mix in lemon juice, paprika, and salt and pepper to taste. Put butter mixture in a shallow bowl and the bread crumbs in another.

Preheat broiler. Use tongs to dip each scallop into the warm butter, then into the bread crumbs, until coated, and arrange them in a single layer on a shallow flameproof dish. Broil the scallops 5 inches from the heat source for 2 minutes, then turn them quickly and broil for another 2 minutes, until the crumbs are golden. Serve scallops and garnish with lemon wedges.

Part Three

GREEN SALADS

Salads have a long history. The most remarkable thing may be that even in ancient times salads were enjoyed essentially as we know them today—raw greens, dressed with oil and seasonings. Lettuce has long been the main ingredient of salads, eaten since at least 800 B.C. Derived from prickly lettuces that grew wild, cultivated lettuce—*Lactuca sativa*—was included in an Assyrian herbal guide listing 250 plants growing in the garden of the king. Lettuce seeds were found in an ancient Egyptian tomb, and there are records of flax and radish-seed oils being used to dress the fresh leaves. The Israelites of the same period ate watercress and lettuce dressed only with salt. Indeed, the very word salad comes from the Latin *sal,* meaning salt.

Chinese records do not seem to mention lettuce until at least 500 A.D., and the first recorded recipe for a salad as we know it may date from 1390, written by King Richard II's master chef. Although he used many more ingredients, his method was similar to ours. His recipe reads, "Take parsley, sage, garlic, Welsh onions, leeks, borage, mint, porette, fennel, watercress, rhue, rosemary, and purslane. Lave them clean, pick them and pluck them small with thine hands and munge (mix) them well with raw olive oil. Lay on vinegar and salt and serve forth."

In North America, lettuce was only one of several greens planted by early colonists. Thomas Jefferson, always far ahead of his time gastronomically, was an avid gardener, and enjoyed not only lettuce and tomatoes but also cucumbers, radishes, parsley, cabbage, celery and sorrel. (Tomatoes, members of the nightshade family, were thought to be poisonous and they were not commonly eaten in the United States until 1825.)

Waverley Root indicates that although lettuce was available in the United States at an early date, it did not become truly popular until after World War I. Today, Boston (or butterhead), iceberg, curly endive, and romaine are our favorite lettuces.

Iceberg lettuce, the most widely available, has inspired heated controversy. Growers and grocers have helped make it popular, since its crisp texture can withstand long transport and temperature change. Gastronomes deplore its lack of taste and subtle character. The late Dione Lucas seethed, "I think all iceberg lettuces should be put into the Atlantic Ocean with the other icebergs." The argument against iceberg lettuces is not restricted to aesthetics: some food authorities point out that a head of iceberg contains one ninth as much vitamin A and one third as much calcium as romaine, and one fourth as much iron as Boston lettuce. Iceberg is perhaps best used in combination with other greens.

There are currently more types of greens widely available than ever before. When composing a salad, choose two to four complementary greens, such as Boston, romaine, watercress, and red-leaf lettuce. Other varieties worth exploring include Belgian endive, leaf lettuce, spinach, escarole, Bibb lettuce, arugula, radicchio, lamb's lettuce, Chinese cabbage and sorrel.

Some food experts claim that a salad should contain only greens; others feel there are no limits to salad ingredients. In any case, a simple green salad must be carefully dressed; the classic vinaigrette or a variation is usually the best choice. Many oils are now widely available, including several olive oils, and those based on corn, safflower, peanut, walnut, hazelnut, sesame, and grape-seed. These can be used alone or in combination. Be sure to buy small quantities, as oils turn rancid quickly. Flavored vinegars have been in vogue recently, though a good French wine vinegar will do just as well. You can, if you like, flavor your own oils and vinegars by steeping fresh herbs, garlic, shallots and other flavoring ingredients in them.

In the past few years we have begun to explore the enormous range of salads from cuisines all over the world. *Crudités,* colorfully arranged bouquets of fresh raw (*cru* in French) vegetables, are now obligatory at every cocktail party. These reflect not only an increased interest in fresh foods, but the realization that food can be made to look as good as it tastes. *Crudités* are offered with a dip or

two, usually based on mayonnaise, yogurt, sour cream, or more unusual mixtures such as puréed avocado or the anchovy-flavored *bagna cauda* (literally, hot bath) of the Piedmont region of Italy.

Mediterranean vegetable stews such as the Provençale *ratatouille* or the pungent Sicilian *caponata* are often served cool as a salad. A few short years ago *ratatouille* was hardly known. Now Americans from coast to coast are not only familiar with this rustic stew, but are often preparing it, as the French do, as a means of using up the produce of their abundant summer gardens.

The *Larousse Gastronomique* separates salads into two groups: simple salads and composed salads. The simple ones are based on one principle ingredient, usually a raw or cooked vegetable.

Everywhere in the world, vegetables of all sorts are tossed with oil and an acid ingredient, such as lemon juice or vinegar, to create salads of amazing diversity. Some vegetables, such as cucumbers, peppers, asparagus and cabbage, seem to lend themselves particularly well to salad treatments.

In Sweden and Denmark, tart cucumber salads known as *gurksallad* and *agurkesalat,* respectively, are often seasoned with fresh dill. The Indians enjoy a salad of cucumbers and peanuts, as well as *khira ka raita,* a cool mixture with a yogurt base. *Cacik, tzatziki,* and *michoteta* are similar mixtures made in Turkey, Greece and other parts of the Middle East. In Japan, cucumbers are tossed with vinegar, sugar, soy sauce and toasted sesame seeds in *kyurimono,* and served with grilled or raw fish.

Eggplant is used in many salads, such as the *ratatouille* and *caponata* already mentioned. Other eggplant salads include the Middle Eastern purée called "poor man's caviar," *simpoog ahgtsan,* an Armenian mixed vegetable salad, the Indian puréed *baingan bhurta,* Szechwan dry-fried eggplant, and Lebanese eggplant with mint and yogurt. These, however, are only a few of the possibilities; Syrians and Turks claim to prepare eggplant in over a thousand ways.

Potatoes, like eggplants, suffered a long period of disfavor before becoming the popular vegetable they are today. Potato salads are extremely varied, including hot versions (such as German potato salad with bacon), cold versions dressed with vinaigrettes or mayonnaise, spicy mixtures such as the *aloo achaar* of Nepal, Indian *batata bhaji* or *alu raita,* and even, in France, the lavish *salade demi-deuil,* a blend of potatoes and costly black truffles.

Beans such as broad white beans and green beans turn up in salads everywhere. The Tuscan combination of white beans and tuna called *fagioli e tonno* is a classic, and so is the Pennsylvania Dutch three-bean salad. Grains, legumes and nuts are transformed into a wide range of salads including French and Middle Eastern lentil salads; white bean salads such as the Egyptian *ful nabed* and *piaz,* Turkish bean salad; *tabbouleh,* based on cracked wheat; an almond salad called *nougada;* and Turkish *tarator* sauce, comprised of walnuts or hazelnuts and crumbled bread. One of the most interesting salads in *fattoush,* a Syrian peasant salad with soaked toasted bread.

Composed salads, or *salades composées,* include several diverse ingredients which are artfully arranged. The most familiar American composed salad is the chef's salad; recently the *salade Niçoise* (with tuna, tomatoes, potatoes and olives) and Greek Salad (*horiatiki,* or village salad, with feta cheese and olives) have appeared on many American menus. Composed salads based on chicken or seafood are found in many cuisines, and classic French cuisine includes such *recherché* versions as the *salade Rossini,* with truffles, and the *salade Ali-Bab,* featuring zucchini, sweet potatoes, shrimps, and nasturtium flowers.

Over the years, some salads have become classics, or have even inspired legends: Hannah Glasse's Salamagundi, an artful arrangement of chicken and vegetables; Caesar's salad, originated in Tijuana; coleslaw; and a New York favorite of the 1960s, fresh spinach salad with bacon, mushrooms, and Parmesan cheese.

Many cuisines have fascinating ways to serve salads. The Indian *raitas,* for example, serve to cool the palate as it is assaulted by highly spiced dishes. Buffets of numerous salads are traditional as hors d'oeuvre, including the Russian *zakouski,* Middle Eastern *mezze,* the *tapas* of Spain, and the full-meal *smörgasbörd* of Scandinavia.

In Japan, salads fall into two groups: *sunomono,* or "vinegared things," and *aemono,* or "dressed, harmonized things." The dressings of the latter are heavier, based on tofu (bean curd), miso (fermented beans), or toasted and ground sesame seeds. These marinated items are served in small portions in elegant bowls as accompaniments to more substantial dishes, or before a meal, with hot sake.

Today our markets offer a wide variety of fresh, leafy greens all year round and, in a way, a crisp green salad has replaced the proverbial daily apple as a requirement to "keep the doctor away." But even so, our awareness of the healthy properties of green salads is not new. The famous herbalist, John Gerard, living in the sixteenth century, said about lettuce that it, "cooleth the heat of the stomach called heartburn, quencheth thirst, and causeth sleep."

Salad Greens

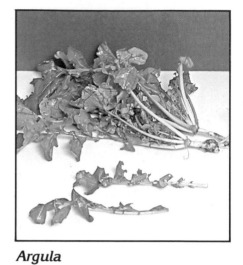

Argula

Belgian Endive

Bibb Lettuce

Chicory

Chinese Cabbage

Lamb's Lettuce

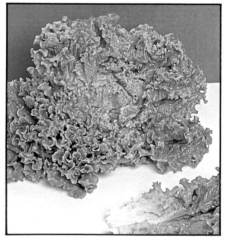

Leaf Lettuce

Romaine

Sorrel and Nasturtium

Boston Lettuce

Cabbage

Escarole

Iceberg Lettuce

Spinach

Watercress

Salads

Salads are food for all seasons, not merely hot-weather or summer fare. The essential characteristic of a salad is freshness. Most of the ingredients are served raw, thereby providing vitamins and minerals that are often lost in cooking. These raw vegetables also offer bulk in the diet.

We are no longer limited to a single kind of head lettuce. All kinds of leafy greens and tender leaves are available in markets and farm stands, and in our own backyards: small plants and herbs can be grown in flowerpots on the back steps or on the windowsill.

Arugula. Also called roquette, rocket, rugula or ruchetta, this is a plant of the mustard family. The taste is pungent, like a sharper watercress. Because of its peppery flavor arugula is most often used in small amounts with other greens.

Belgian Endive. This creamy-white, cigar-shaped plant is 4 to 6 inches long, with a crisp texture and delicately bitter flavor. All of the endive is edible, but it is best to trim the base and cut out a cone-shaped piece, as this portion is particularly bitter. Available from September through May.

Bibb Lettuce. A kind of butterhead lettuce, dark green and crisp, with a delicate flavor. The heads are small and remain crisp longer than most salad greens.

Boston Lettuce. Butterhead lettuce, with loose, soft, pale-green leaves, is a fine all-purpose lettuce.

Cabbage. Round-head green and red cabbages and the pointed-head, crinkly-leaved Savoy cabbage are all good for salads. Discard coarse outer leaves, cut head into quarters, and cut out the core. Slice across the quarters to make fine shreds.

Chicory. The very curly leaves are deep green on the outside, fading to bleached pale yellow in the center. They can be used alone, but because of their somewhat bitter taste, they are generally mixed with milder greens or used as a garnish.

Chinese Cabbage. There are at least 4 different kinds. The one used raw is called celery cabbage and has a delicate flavor. The yellow-white leaves have a celerylike rib tapering to the top. Leaves are firm, crisp, densely packed. Delicious served raw and often used as a substitute for romaine.

Escarole. The slightly bitter taste is good combined with other salad greens, and is also delicious cooked.

Iceberg Lettuce. The heads, which store well and retain crispness, are large and firm, with tightly packed, medium-green leaves. America's most popular lettuce; available 12 months.

Lamb's Lettuce. Also known as field salad and corn salad. A spring and summer plant, with dark-green, tongue-shaped or spoon-shaped leaves. It has a tangy taste, especially delicious when the plants are young, and tender. Can be used like lettuce.

Leaf Lettuces. These loose-leaved or bunching lettuces produce a profusion of leaves but do not form heads. They have delicate flavor, and the firm but succulent texture provides a pleasant contrast when mixed with coarser greens.

Romaine. The elongated head is made of loosely packed green leaves 6 to 8 inches in length. The midribs are heavy; the outer leaves are dark green

Preparing Salad Greens

1 Trim off stem end of head and discard any wilted or bruised outer leaves.

2 Separate leaves: remove any tough ribs or stems and any woody core.

3 Wash leaves thoroughly in a sink or large bowl of room-temperature water.

4 Wash again in a bowl of fresh water if leaves are very sandy. Shake leaves to drain.

5 Shake in a salad basket, or spin in a salad dryer, or drain in a colander, until leaves are just damp.

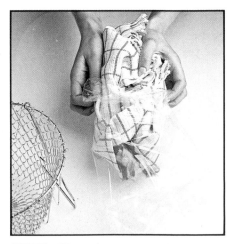

6 Wrap damp leaves in a clean cloth towel and slide into a plastic bag. Chill for up to 1 hour.

and tend to be coarse. There is a pleasant hint of bitterness in this green. This is a must for Caesar's salad.

Sorrel and Nasturtium. The strong lemony taste of these leaves add a delicious tartness and pungency to salads. Small whole leaves can be used for garnish.

Spinach. Available all year round. Fresh spinach is a popular salad green. Look for leaves that are fresh, dark green, without insect holes, decay spots or slimy surfaces. Wash thoroughly in room-temperature water, pull off the stems, and wash again.

Watercress. This pungent green offers a peppery accent to salads, in addition to the attractive appearance of their dark-green, round leaves. Wash by immersing in cool water. The stems have a more intense flavor than the leaves, so discard most of them before adding to a salad.

Preparing the Salad Greens

• *Choose a variety of greens.* Simplicity in a salad is a virtue, but dullness is not. Try to select 2 or 3 different greens with thought to color, texture and taste. Even the familiar iceberg lettuce can be enhanced with the addition of watercress and tender leaves of Boston or Bibb lettuce.

• *Wash the salad greens well.* The prettiest lettuces and the freshest greens are recent arrivals from the farm so that their leaves inevitably conceal some flecks of garden dirt and sandy grit. Discard any tough or bruised outer leaves. Use plenty of cool water to wash the leaves. This can be a time-consuming task but it is well worth doing carefully.

• *Dry the greens well.* Dripping wet salad greens will turn soggy in no time at all, and the dressing will run off. Use a salad spinner; twirl a salad basket; or gently roll your greens up in a fluffy bath towel.

• *Plan ahead.* You can wash and dry your greens early in the day and be ready to prepare a salad in minutes. Place the clean, dry greens in a plastic bag and store in the refrigerator for up to 2 days. There are those who feel that salad greens should always be cooled for an hour or so in order to be perfectly crisp.

Salad Dressing

A classic vinaigrette is the basic dressing for simple green salads. The ingredients are the best-quality oil you can find and afford, a good wine vinegar, salt and pepper.

• *Oil.* Olive oil is the most popular choice. There are many varieties to choose from; try several to find the one you like best. Imported olive oils that are labeled "first pressing" and/or "virgin" are the most aromatic and flavorful. The greenish gold oils imported from Greece and Sicily have a strong olive flavor and intense fruity aroma.

Using Garlic

1 For a mild garlic flavor, halve the peeled clove and rub the cut side on the inside of the salad bowl. Discard garlic.

2 For garlic-flavored dressing, quarter the clove and drop into dressing. Leave for 1 hour, then remove and discard garlic.

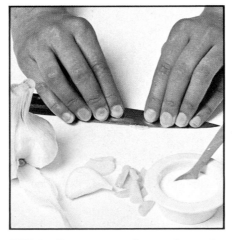

3 For a stronger flavor, slice garlic, sprinkle with salt, and crush with a knife blade. Add the pulp to the prepared dressing.

OR Push the peeled clove through a garlic press. Add puréed pulp to the dressing. Discard any fibers in the press.

Other oils from France and Italy have a more delicate flavor and fragrance. All good olive oil is expensive, but it is truly the "secret ingredient" in a delicious green salad.

Safflower and sunflower oils are popular for their light, bland taste. They are excellent mixed in equal proportions with olive oil for a lighter flavor.

Walnut or hazelnut oils (the best are imported from France) impart a delicate nutty taste and are especially delicious with the sturdier greens such as arugula, chicory and watercress. These oils are perishable and should be stored in the refrigerator.

• *Vinegar.* A good wine vinegar (white and red) should be a staple in your cupboard since it is essential to a vinaigrette dressing. You may also wish to try some of the many other vinegars that have become available recently. There are vinegars flavored with herbs and others flavored with berries. Japanese rice vinegar is somewhat less acid and has a pleasant slightly sweet taste. Aged sherry vinegar has mellow, nutty flavor. Balsamic vinegar from Italy is enjoying great popularity; it is very dark, almost syrupy, and has a rich, heavy sweetness. Use it with a light hand or it will overwhelm a delicate salad.

• *Salt.* Although we do not normally think of it, salt, too, has texture and flavor. Kosher salt has a pure, clean taste that is more interesting than ordinary table salt and the coarse grains are slow to dissolve, ensuring a longer lasting crispness in the salad. Sea salt crystals can be freshly ground like peppercorns and they impart a sharp, tangy taste of the sea.

• *Pepper.* Black or white peppercorns should be freshly ground and incorporated into the dressing or passed in a peppermill at table.

• *Lemon juice.* Freshly squeezed lemon juice, strained through a sieve to remove pits and pulp, may be substituted for the vinegar in a vinaigrette. The result is a dressing that is pleasantly tart, with a brisk, citrus flavor.

• *Herbs.* Ideally, only fresh herbs should find their way into a dressing for a crisp green salad. Parsley, dill, tarragon, basil, chervil and chives are all agreeable additions to a vinaigrette.

• *Garlic.* Some people can't abide it and others can't live without it. Fortunately a good green salad can stand alone or happily incorporate enough garlic to please the most ardent afficionado.

• *Shallots and Scallions.* A minced shallot is an excellent addition to a vinaigrette and a piquant alternative to garlic. Scallions, all the white ends and some of the green, also chopped fine, are delicious and seem to go particularly well with a tart, lemony dressing.

• *Mustard.* A pinch of dry mustard or a scant teaspoon of Dijon-style prepared mustard may be added to a standard vinaigrette.

• *Other Flavorings:*
A bit of anchovy paste.
Some crumbled blue or feta cheese.
A generous grating of Parmesan or Asiago cheese.
A dollop of sour cream.

Vinaigrette Dressing

Makes ¼ cup

1 tablespoon wine vinegar
   salt
   freshly ground pepper
4 tablespoons olive oil

A food processor is ideal for making a vinaigrette dressing. If you are adding fresh herbs, mince the desired quantity in the food processor bowl, then add the other ingredients. Turn the processor on and off 2 or 3 times.

1 Measure the vinegar into a small bowl or cup, or use a jar with a tight-fitting cover.

2 Add salt and pepper to taste and stir until salt is dissolved in the vinegar.

3 Pour in the oil and beat vigorously to mix and thicken; or if you have a jar, fasten the cover and shake to mix.

A hard-cooked egg yolk pressed through a sieve.

Assembling the Salad

• *Prepare the dressing.* This may be done a little ahead (up to an hour) but as "freshness" is the keyword in this type of salad, the vinaigrette should not sit around for hours. Do not refrigerate because the oil will solidify to an unpleasant texture.

• *Prepare the greens.* Remove the crisp, clean, dry greens from the refrigerator and tear them into bite-size pieces with your hands. Place them in a large salad bowl.

• *Toss the Salad.* Add the dressing to the greens and toss, making sure that every leaf gets its fair share of dressing. Experts continue to debate the question of whether it is better to use your hands or the normal implements. The choice is yours, but do it just before you serve the salad.

Vegetables and Other Ingredients for Salads

All sorts of vegetables or other ingredients can be added to the greens, or can be used without greens for delicious salads. These are some of the most familiar.

Alfalfa Sprouts. Beautiful as a decoration or as an ingredient. Use raw. Available in most supermarkets, but they are simple to sprout at home.

Preparing a Green Salad

1 If you like mild garlic flavor, rub the cut side of half a garlic clove round the inside of the bowl.

2 Put salad vegetables (according to season) in the bowl.

3 Scatter mustard and cress or fresh herbs evenly over the other ingredients.

4 Make vinaigrette or any other dressing of your choice and beat well.

5 Pour over the salad. Do not use too much—just enough to coat lightly.

6 Use your hands or salad servers to toss ingredients and coat evenly. Serve the salad immediately.

1 *Avocados:* Using a stainless-steel knife, halve the fruit and remove pit. Prepare just before serving.

2 Brush cut surfaces with lemon to prevent browning. Fill cavities; or peel, slice, dice, or cut balls; add to salads.

1 *Cucumbers:* Trim ends and peel. Slice on mandoline or in a food processor.

1 *Carrots:* Young carrots have the best flavor; old carrots can be hard and less sweet. Scrub well; scrape; trim ends.

2 Use box grater, food processor or mill. Shred in processor or food grinder. Slice, chop, or cut into julienne.

1 *Fennel:* Trim off the base of the bulb, any coarse or browning outer layers, and all the stems.

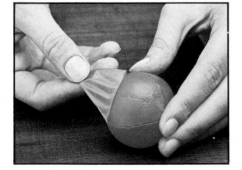

1 *Tomatoes:* Blanch and peel by dropping into boiling water for 1 minute; lift out; plunge into cold water. Nick skin; pull it off.

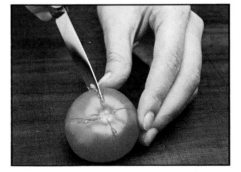

2 Cut out core. Cut tomatoes into quarters or wedges; slice or chop. Gently press out seeds, if desired.

1 *Peppers:* Red or green can be used. Wash, halve and remove the stalk, pith and seeds.

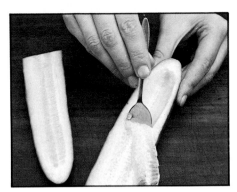

 If seeds are mature, halve cucumbers and scoop out. Salting makes cucumbers limp.

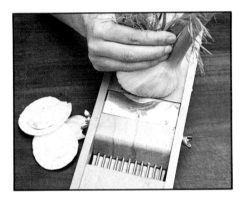

2 Reserve leaves for garnish. Stems can be used for fish stock. Slice, shred, chop, or cut fennel into julienne.

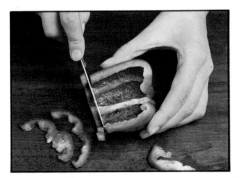

2 Peppers can be sliced either horizontally or vertically into thin strips.

Avocado. A buttery, pale-green fruit, good for color and delicate taste. These discolor when exposed to air, so brush cut surfaces with lemon or lime juice.

Beans. The thinnest, youngest green snap beans may be used raw. Otherwise they should be blanched in boiling water and cooled.

Bean Sprouts. These can be used raw or blanched in boiling water for 1 minute.

Broccoli. Raw broccoli is excellent in salads, but it may be cooked briefly as well. Separate the head into florets. Trim, peel, and slice the stalk.

Carrots. Scrub, scrape and trim them, and grate, chop, slice, or cut into julienne for colorful and nutritious additions to salad.

Cauliflower. This is delicious raw. Separate the head into florets. Shortly before you use them, sprinkle them with coarse salt and let them soak in cold water for 10 minutes. Drain, rinse, and drain again. Also good slivered.

Celery Knob. Scrub it, peel it, cut into slices, then into julienne strips.

Cucumber. Tender, garden-grown cucumbers can be used without peeling or scooping out the seeds. Commercial varieties, when coated with a wax, should be peeled. If the seeds have developed into hardshells they must be scooped out. Cucumbers can be chopped, diced, grated. They make an excellent first-course salad, hollowed out and filled with flavorful mixtures.

Fennel. This licorice-flavored vegetable is delicious as a salad ingredient, and the feathery leaves make an excellent garnish.

Mushrooms. Stems are best set aside for other uses, as they are less tender. Do not peel mushrooms unless they are very soiled or damaged. Just wipe them with a damp paper towel

and let them dry completely. Slice them. They are delicious with a dressing of lemon juice and olive oil and a sprinkling of herbs.

Onions. All sorts of onions can be used in salads—yellow onions, red onions, white Bermuda onions, Spanish onions, shallots, scallions, chives. Use rings of large onions, tiny rings of scallions, minced shallots, snipped chives.

Peas. The new Sugar Snap peas may be eaten whole, including the pods, and they are delicious raw. Other peas should be shelled and added raw or briefly blanched.

Peppers. Bell peppers, red and green, Italian peppers and many small mild peppers can be used in salads. Bell peppers are always better when peeled. Roast them to char the skin, or simply peel with a vegetable peeler. Discard stems, ribs and seeds.

Radishes. Red, white and black radishes can be used for salads. Choose plump and crisp radishes, red ones should be smooth and without blemishes, as the color is good in salads. Black radishes should be peeled. Slice or grate.

Tomatoes. Splendid salad vegetables when they are in season and have been ripened on the vine. They may be peeled and seeded before adding them to the salad or they may simply be washed, dried and sliced.

Zucchini. These squashes are as delicious raw as cucumbers. Slice, chop or grate.

Preparing Salad Vegetables

A food processor is a perfect machine to prepare anything that needs to be sliced, chopped, shredded, grated. Lacking that, use a madoline; or simply slice and chop with a sharp chef's knife

64

Dicing

 1 Cut vegetable to fit feed tube. Proceed to process with spiral disc in place.

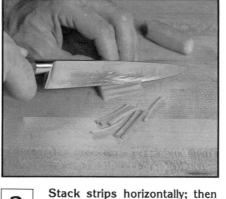

2 Holding securely with fingers, chop crosswise to make dice.

Processor Shredding

1 Cut vegetable (carrots shown here) into slices. Stack and cut into lengthwise strips.

Julienne

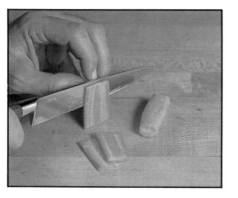

 1 Cut vegetable into thin lengthwise strips.

2 Stack strips horizontally; then cut through each stack, making matchstick strips.

Mincing

1 Bunch washed vegetables or herbs tightly. Grip knife firmly in hand and slice through leaves. Gather into a mound.

Slicing and Chopping

1 Peel onion. With a sharp chopping knife, cut the onion from top to bottom into halves.

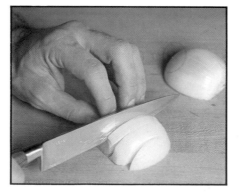

2 Put onion, cut side down, on board. Make lengthwise slices at regular intervals, cutting down but not through root end.

 3 Hold sliced onion half by root end. Cut horizontally to—*but not through*—the root end.

on a sturdy board. A swivel vegetable peeler is perfect for peeling everything, and can also be used to slice or sliver hard vegetables such as carrots. A melon baller can be used to make neat little rounds.

Garnishes

Even a simple home meal for two can seem like a banquet if everything is presented beautifully. The portions of various foods should be balanced with each other, and the plate should be chosen well for its size and color. A contrast of color and texture is essen-

2 Holding knife against chopping board—and without lifting tip—cut across mound using rocking motion to achieve desired mince.

4 To chop, hold sliced onion with fingertips curled under, knife blade against them; cut downward completely through slices.

tial for a good meal. The final touch may be a perfect garnish.

The most usual garnish is a sprig of parsley, and there's nothing wrong with that, but it must be a perfect, glossy, green leafy sprig that one can pick up and eat with pleasure. Other similar choices might be Chinese parsley sprigs, watercress sprigs, tiny celery leaves. Wash the sprigs, roll gently in a towel to dry; add to dish at the last moment. In addition, any of these little greens can be minced for a different kind of garnish.

Most vegetable and fruit garnishes are made from raw ingredients, but hard root vegetables such as beets, turnips, potatoes, etc., must be fully cooked or at least blanched.

More elaborate garnishes are good for parties. The work is not difficult but does require dexterity and you will need sharp knives, a swivel vegetable peeler, a citrus zester, an apple corer, a melon baller with 2 sizes of scoops, and if possible truffle cutters and other sharp cutters of various shapes.

- *Brushes or Fringes.* Cut lengths of celery rib or scallion vertically almost to the base to make many little slivers. Drop the vegetables into ice water to make the fringes open out and curl. Use to garnish sandwiches and salads.

- *Chiffonade.* This is a garnish of leafy vegetables or herbs, cut into thin shreds. Roll up several leaves into a cigar shape, and cut across into narrow strips. Shake out the strips. A fine garnish for soups.

- *Chrysanthemums.* Use firm round white onions and cut them from top to base into slivers, leaving the slivers still attached at the base. Drop into ice water and let the slivers open out.

- *Curls.* Cut paper-thin slices from carrots or rutabagas, curl up the slices, fasten with a food pick, and drop into ice water.

- *Julienne Strips.* These can be cut from any firm vegetable. Parboil all root vegetables, or any that are hard to eat

raw. Make thin slices, then cut these into strips no thicker than a matchstick.

- *Roses.* Cut these from radishes; make petal-shaped cuts from top to near the base, all around; if the radish is large enough, make a second row of cuts inside the first. Drop into ice water to encourage the roses to open.

- *Shapes.* Cut these from raw carrots or cucumbers, or from blanched beets, turnips or rutabagas. Use truffle or cookie cutters.

- *Twists.* These can be made from paper-thin slices of orange, lemon or cucumber. Make a cut from outside to the center of the slice and twist the slice.

Skewered Tidbits

At party time small skewers of vegetables and other foods can serve as nibbles. These are nutritious without being fattening and they do not jade the appetite as many other cocktail foods can do. Serve them in a "hedgehog" made of a large firm cabbage, a grapefruit or a pineapple. Stick small skewers into the cabbage to make "spines."

Use pieces of celery and whole black grapes sandwiched together with cream cheese.

Curl strips of smoked salmon around marinated mushrooms.

Cut cooked beets into pretty shapes and thread on the skewer with pickled pearl onions and small orange segments.

Fill pitted dates with cream cheese. Thread on sticks and top with a carrot curl.

Brush melon and avocado balls with lemon juice and thread on sticks with green grapes.

Edible garnishes are especially appealing to children and will enliven any birthday party or special occasion. Children also enjoy creating them so don't hesitate to enlist their aid when you need a large supply of carrot curls, orange twists, melon balls and other vegetable fancies.

Edible Garnishes

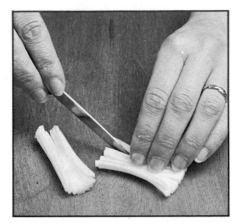

1 *Brushes or fringes:* Slit one end of a 2-inch piece of celery or scallion into narrow strips.

2 If using celery, repeat with the other end, leaving the center uncut to hold all together.

3 Immerse in ice water for 1 hour, until fringed ends have curled. Drain and serve immediately.

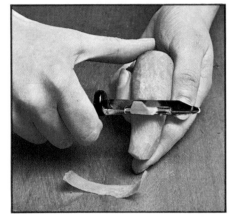

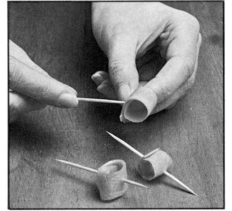

1 *Curls:* Using a vegetable peeler, cut a long thin strip from a peeled carrot or parboiled rutabaga.

2 Roll up gently; pierce with a sharply pointed cocktail stick to secure.

3 Immerse the curls in a large bowl of ice water for 1 hour. Drain, remove picks, and serve.

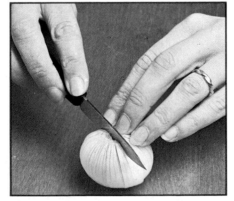

1 *Chrysanthemums:* Cut a peeled round onion into quarters, stopped just short of the base.

2 Now cut again into 8 sections, then into 16 sections, each time stopping short of the base.

3 Open the petals with your fingers. Immerse in ice water for 1 hour, drain, and serve immediately.

1 *Turned mushrooms:* Make skin-deep cuts ¼ inch apart from the center top to the edge.

2 Repeat the process, turning the knife in the other direction but following the same curve.

3 Pull away the narrow strips of skin between the cuts to give a fluted effect.

1 *Twists:* Wipe skins of orange, lemon or cucumber; do not peel. Cut paper-thin slices.

2 Using a sharp knife, make a cut from the center to the edge of the slice.

3 Hold the slice at each side of the cut and twist in opposite directions.

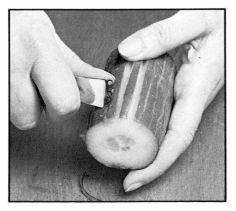

1 *Shapes:* Use a lemon zester to score the sides of an unpeeled cucumber.

2 Cut cucumber into thin slices. Slices will have an attractive serrated edge.

3 Use truffle or aspic cutters to stamp out shapes from various vegetables, truffles, pimientos or aspic sheets.

English Salad Cream

makes 1¼ cups

2 hard-cooked egg yolks
pinch of salt
pinch of cayenne pepper
1 teaspoon dry mustard

1 teaspoon superfine
granulated sugar
2 tablespoons white-wine
vinegar
1 cup heavy cream

Push the cold egg yolks through a sieve into a bowl. With a wooden spoon, mix salt, cayenne, mustard and sugar into the yolks. Add 1 teaspoon of the vinegar and mix well. Gradually add the cream, stirring lightly all the time. Finally blend in remaining vinegar.

Blue Cheese Dressing

makes 1¼ cups

½ cup small-curd cottage
cheese
¼ cup buttermilk
2 tablespoons white-wine
vinegar

2 ounces blue cheese
freshly ground black
pepper

Push cottage cheese through a fine sieve. Stir in buttermilk and wine vinegar. Crumble the blue cheese (there will be about ½ cup) and mash it. Mix with other ingredients until well blended. Season lightly with pepper.

Tahini Dressing

makes about ¾ cup

3 tablespoons tahini (sesame
seed paste)
6 tablespoons cold water
1 garlic clove

fresh lemon juice
2 teaspoons minced fresh
parsley
paprika

Combine tahini and cold water; stir well until blended. Peel garlic and put through a press into the tahini mixture. Add lemon juice to taste and the minced parsley. Add a light sprinkling of paprika and mix again.

Buttermilk Cucumber Dressing

makes about 1 cup

1 small cucumber
½ cup buttermilk
3 tablespoons cream cheese
2 teaspoons lemon juice

1 teaspoon snipped fresh dill
¼ teaspoon salt
freshly ground white
pepper

Peel cucumber and cut into 1-inch pieces. Purée cucumber, buttermilk, cream cheese, lemon juice, dill, salt, and pepper to taste in a food processor or blender until smooth. Chill, covered, for 30 minutes before serving. Delicious on seafood salads and tomatoes.

Yogurt and Honey Dressing

makes 1¼ cups

juice of ½ lemon
1 teaspoon clear honey
1 cup plain yogurt
1 garlic clove

salt and pepper
1 tablespoon chopped fresh
mint leaves

Mix lemon juice and honey in a small bowl. Gradually blend in the yogurt. Peel and slice garlic and crush it with a little salt. Stir garlic into the dressing and season with pepper to taste. Add mint. A good dressing for salads of cucumber, tomato, and various root vegetables.

Sweet-and-Sour Dressing

makes ½ cup

2 tablespoons sesame seeds
3 tablespoons cider vinegar
1 tablespoon soft brown
sugar
2 tablespoons soy sauce

freshly ground black
pepper
2 tablespoons sunflower,
corn, or peanut oil

Pound sesame seeds in a mortar or put them in a plastic bag and crush with a rolling pin. Stir vinegar into sugar. Add crushed seeds, soy sauce, and pepper to taste. Mix well, then stir in the oil and shake or stir to blend.

Tomato Sour-Cream Dressing

makes 1½ cups

2 tomatoes, about 8 ounces
1 cup dairy sour cream
1 teaspoon paprika

1 tablespoon chopped fresh
basil or marjoram
salt and white pepper

Cover tomatoes with boiling water in a bowl or saucepan and leave for 2 minutes. Lift out to a bowl of cold water. Peel tomatoes, chop roughly, and rub through a coarse sieve to salads made with oranges or other citrus fruits, onions, and watercress.

Marmalade Dressing

makes ⅓ cup

1 tablespoon orange juice
1 teaspoon grated orange
rind
2 tablespoons marmalade

pinch of sea salt
freshly ground black
pepper
¼ cup olive oil

Stir orange juice and grated rind into the marmalade. Add salt and pepper to taste. Using a fork, stir in the olive oil until dressing is well mixed. Adjust seasoning if necessary. Use for remove all seeds. Gradually blend in the sour cream, paprika and chopped herb. Use for shellfish salads and those made with vegetables such as green beans.

Avocado Dressing

makes 1½ cups

1 ripe avocado
1 small onion
2 tablespoons fresh lemon
    juice

⅓ cup plain yogurt
⅛ teaspoon salt
    freshly ground pepper
¼ teaspoon Tabasco®

Peel avocado, discard pit, and cut the fruit into small pieces. Peel and quarter the onion. Process avocado, onion, lemon juice and yogurt in a food processor or blender with 3 or 4 on and off motions, until smooth. Stir in salt, pepper to taste, and Tabasco.

Without a blender or processor, mash avocado with a fork until quite smooth. Sprinkle with lemon juice. Mince the onion. Stir onion and other ingredients into mashed avocado until smooth.

Tarragon Cream Dressing

makes about 1 cup

1 teaspoon superfine
    granulated sugar
    pinch of salt
    freshly ground black
    pepper

2 tablespoons tarragon
    vinegar
1 cup light cream

Put sugar, salt and plenty of pepper in a small bowl. Pour in the vinegar and stir well with a fork. Add the cream gradually, stirring with light movements of the fork so dressing thickens

slightly. Taste for seasoning and blend in a little more vinegar if necessary. Use for salads made of cucumber, cabbage and lettuce.

Salade Verte
(Green Salad)

4 portions

1 head of Boston or romaine
    lettuce or curly chicory
1 bunch of watercress
    few leaves of lamb's
    lettuce, dandelion and
    sorrel, as available

    salt and pepper
4 tablespoons olive oil
4 teaspoons white-wine
    vinegar

Break up large salad leaves, leaving small leaves whole. Remove any yellowing leaves from watercress and discard tough stems from watercress and sorrel. Wash all the greens in cool water, drain well, and shake off as much of remaining

drops as possible. Roll the greens in a cloth towel and then in plastic wrap and crisp in the refrigerator for 1 hour.

Place dry greens in a salad bowl, season to taste, and pour in oil and vinegar. Toss until all the leaves are coated with the dressing.

Italian Green Salad

6 portions

1 large head of romaine	3 tablespoons minced fresh parsley
3 small zucchini	3 tablespoons raw fresh peas
1 small green pepper	salt and black pepper
1 fennel heart	3 tablespoons Vinaigrette
1 tablespoon minced fresh basil	Dressing (see Index)

Separate romaine leaves, remove thick ribs from the leaves, and wash thoroughly. Cut or tear the large leaves into smaller pieces. Roll lettuce in a towel to dry. Wash and trim zucchini; without peeling them, cut into thin slices. Wash the pepper, remove stem, ribs and seeds, and cut pepper into thin strips.

Trim the fennel and shred it. Place the vegetables in a salad bowl and sprinkle in the herbs and the peas. Mix gently and season lightly. Just before serving, toss in the dressing; use more dressing if you prefer.

72

Spinach and Cheese Salad

6 portions

1	pound fresh spinach	6	ounces Edam or Gouda cheese or other firm, mild cheese
2	shallots		
4	tablespoons olive oil	3	hard-cooked egg yolks
2	tablespoons fresh lemon juice		salt and pepper

Wash spinach thoroughly. Pull off the stems. Set any large leaves aside for another use and roll all the small leaves in a towel to dry. Peel shallots and mince almost to a purée. Stir shallots into the oil and mix with lemon juice; set aside. Cut cheese into tiny cubes, about the size of a dried bean. Push

the egg yolks through a sieve into a small bowl.

Toss spinach and cheese together. Add salt sparingly as cheese is salty. Add as much pepper as you like. Pour in the dressing and toss well. Finally, sprinkle the sieved egg yolk over the top. Serve promptly, while spinach is still crisp.

Cabbage and Apple Salad

4 to 6 portions

8	ounces Savoy cabbage (about half of a small head)	4	green onions (scallions)
		¼	cup mayonnaise
2	firm red-skinned apples (Stayman, Winesap, Delicious)	¼	cup Vinaigrette Dressing (see Index)
		2	tablespoons minced fresh chervil or parsley

Trim the cabbage and shred it by hand or in a mandoline. Wash the apples but do not peel them; remove stems, cores and blossom ends, and cut apples from top to bottom into thin slivers. Trim green onions and cut both white and green parts into thin rings. Toss these ingredients together in a

large bowl. Combine mayonnaise and vinaigrette, and pour into the salad; toss well. Taste; you may want to add more salt and pepper than the dressing provides. Sprinkle minced herb on top. This salad can wait in a cool place for about 30 minutes before serving, as cabbage does not wilt.

Chick-pea and Spinach Salad with Yogurt

4 to 6 portions

6	ounces dried chick-peas		salt and pepper
1	pound fresh spinach	½	cup plain yogurt
6	tablespoons olive oil	2	tablespoons chopped parsley
2	tablespoons wine vinegar		

Soak chick-peas in cold water overnight. Lift from the soaking water to a large saucepan and add about 4 cups fresh water. Bring to a boil, cover, and simmer gently for 1½ hours, or until peas are tender but not mushy. Let them cool in the cooking liquid, then drain. (Cooking liquid can be saved for soup.)

Wash spinach, discard any coarse or damaged leaves,

and pull off all the stems. Cut large leaves into pieces; leave small leaves whole. Combine chick-peas and spinach in a salad bowl. Pour in oil and vinegar, and add salt and pepper to taste. Toss everything together, but gently so as not to break up the peas. Chill the salad until ready to serve.

Add serving time, arrange the mixture in a shallow bowl and top with yogurt. Sprinkle parsley over all.

Variations: Add some raw onion rings, from a mild onion. If you like garlic, add a crushed clove to the oil before mixing it into the salad.

Grapefruit and Sesame Salad

4 portions

1	small head of lettuce	8	teaspoons sesame seeds
2	large grapefruits	4	tablespoons watercress leaves
4	tablespoons tahini (sesame paste)		

Trim, wash, and drain the lettuce. Roll in a towel to dry and chill in the refrigerator for 30 minutes. Shred the lettuce and divide among 4 salad plates.

Cut peel and pith from grapefruits and separate the fruits into segments. For a perfect salad, remove the membrane from the segments. Arrange grapefruit on top of the lettuce. Spoon tahini over grapefruit and scatter sesame seeds on top. Garnish with watercress leaves.

Note: If your tahini is very thick, thin it to the right consistency with a little peanut oil and a little lemon juice.

Orange and Olive Salad

4 portions

1 bunch of watercress
2 large oranges
20 pitted black olives

⅓ cup Marmalade Dressing or
Vinaigrette Dressing (see Index)
4 thin slices of Bermuda onion or other mild-flavored onion

Wash watercress, discard most of the stems, and cut leafy portions into small bouquets. Drain and dry watercress. Grate the orange rind to use in the marmalade dressing, or to add to the vinaigrette. Carefully remove white portion of orange peel and cut the fruit into slices; quarter the slices and remove any pits. Combine watercress, orange pieces and olives in a salad bowl. Pour in the dressing and toss to mix well. Separate the onion slices into rings and arrange on top of the salad. Serve at once.

Agurkesalat

(Danish Cucumber Salad)

4 portions

3 cucumbers
4 teaspoons salt
½ cup white vinegar
1 tablespoon lemon juice

1 tablespoon sugar
¼ teaspoon white pepper
3 tablespoons snipped fresh dill

Wash cucumbers, score skin from end to end, and cut them into thin slices. Put slices in a shallow bowl and sprinkle with 3 teaspoons of the salt. Set aside, covered, for 2 hours.

Combine vinegar, lemon juice, sugar, pepper and remaining teaspoon of salt; stir until sugar and salt are dissolved.

Remove cucumber slices from the bowl, rinse, and press between kitchen towels to remove as much liquid as possible. Arrange slices in a serving dish. Pour vinegar dressing over and sprinkle with fresh dill. Chill for 1 hour before serving.

Cabbage and Pepper Salad

8 portions

1 red bell pepper
1 green bell pepper
6 green onions (scallions)
1 cucumber
1 pound tomatoes
8 ounces white cabbage
¾ cup salad oil

¼ cup vinegar
2 tablespoons honey
juice of 1 lemon
2 teaspoons salt
1 teaspoons freshly ground black pepper

Wash peppers, remove stems, ribs and seeds, and cut peppers from top to bottom into thin strips. Trim green onions and shred them. Wash and peel cucumber and cut into ½-inch cubes. Wash tomatoes, peel if desired, and slice them. Trim the cabbage and shred it with a chef's knife to fine strips. Combine all the vegetables in a large bowl and chill for 30 minutes.

Combine remaining ingredients in a screw-top jar and shake until well mixed. Pour dressing over vegetables just before serving. Toss well to coat pieces with dressing.

Apple Salad with Watercress and Radishes

4 portions

2 tart dessert apples
1 bunch of watercress
3 ounces red radishes
4 celery ribs
2 ounces raisins
    celery leaves, for garnish

¼ cup olive oil
2 tablespoons cider vinegar
1 teaspoon prepared
    Dijon-style mustard
1 garlic clove
    salt and pepper

Wash and core apples and cut into thin slices. Wash watercress, discard most of the stems, and chop the rest. Wash and trim radishes and slice. Trim and chop celery ribs. Combine all the vegetables and the raisins in a salad bowl. Wash and dry the celery leaves for garnish, and cut into small bouquets.

Make the dressing: Beat together the oil, vinegar and mustard. Peel garlic and put through a press into the dressing. Season to taste. Pour dressing over salad, and toss well. Garnish with celery leaves and serve at once.

Coleslaw

6 portions

1	pound round-head or Savoy cabbage
2	celery ribs
1	small onion
2	ounces shelled walnuts
2	ounces golden raisins

5	tablespoons mayonnaise or English Salad Cream (see Index)
2	teaspoons white vinegar or lemon juice
	freshly ground black pepper

Remove any ragged outer leaves from the cabbage. Cut into quarters and discard the stalk. Shred cabbage into a large bowl. Wash and trim celery and chop into small pieces. Peel and chop the onion. Add both to the cabbage. Chop walnuts and add them to the bowl along with the raisins.

Put the mayonnaise or salad cream in a small bowl. Add vinegar and black pepper to taste and mix well. Pour the dressing over the salad and toss lightly. Cover and chill for about 30 minutes before serving.

Asinan
(Balinese Green Salad)

6 to 8 portions

½ head of Chinese cabbage	2 tablespoons white-wine vinegar
1 small head of lettuce	1 teaspoon granulated sugar
½ long thin cucumber	½ teaspoon cayenne pepper
1 pound bean sprouts from mung beans	salt
5 tablespoons sesame or safflower oil	6 slices bacon
	2 tablespoons roasted peanuts

Wash cabbage and lettuce, shake dry, and wrap in a towel, then in a plastic bag. Chill for 30 minutes.

Shred cabbage and lettuce; set lettuce aside for later; put cabbage in a large salad bowl. Peel cucumber and cut into 2-inch strips. Add cucumber and bean sprouts to cabbage. Make the dressing: Blend the 5 tablespoons of oil and the vinegar and stir in sugar, cayenne pepper, and salt to taste until sugar and salt are dissolved. Pour dressing into the salad and set aside to chill.

Fry bacon until crisp. Transfer to paper towels to drain and cool, then crumble and sprinkle over the salad.

Arrange the shredded lettuce in a large salad bowl and spoon the dressed salad on top. Chop the peanuts and scatter over the top for a final garnish.

Gruyère and Mushroom Salad

4 portions

8 ounces Gruyère cheese	1 garlic clove
4 ounces fresh mushrooms	salt and pepper
6 tablespoons olive oil	4 large lettuce leaves
6 tablespoons red-wine vinegar	1 tablespoon minced fresh parsley

Cut Gruyère into ½-inch cubes. Trim mushroom stems and wipe caps with a damp cloth. Quarter the mushrooms. Combine cheese and mushrooms in a medium-size bowl. Whisk olive oil and wine vinegar together. Peel garlic clove and put through a press into the dressing. Add salt and pepper to taste. Pour dressing over cheese and mushrooms, toss to coat pieces well, and set aside to marinate for 30 minutes.

To serve, line the bottom of a shallow salad bowl or 4 individual plates with the lettuce leaves. Arrange the dressed cheese and mushrooms on the lettuce. Sprinkle with parsley. Serve promptly. This salad tastes better when it is at room temperature rather than very cold.

Dandelion and Bacon Salad

4 portions

1 pound fresh dandelion leaves	4 tablespoons olive oil
8 slices of bacon	1 tablespoon red-wine vinegar
8 cherry tomatoes	salt and pepper

Wash dandelion leaves; remove roots and coarse outer leaves. If leaves are long, cut them into shorter lengths. Roll the tender leaves in a towel to dry. Cook bacon until crisp and transfer to paper towels to drain. Crumble bacon.

Combine dandelion leaves and tomatoes in a salad bowl. Pour in oil and vinegar. Add very little salt, as bacon is salty, and pepper to taste. Toss well to mix all together. Sprinkle crumbled bacon on top and serve.

Part Four
CAKES

In the past, the preparation of cakes was the concern of professional pastry chefs. This is still true in France, where the branch of cooking known as *pâtisserie* has elevated the craft of cakes and pastries to a fine art. Austrian and Hungarian pastries are also regarded as among the finest in the world.

Over the years, cake baking moved from the realm of professional cooks to that of the home baker. This was particularly true in America, where cakes became a culinary specialty. As the tempo of modern life increased and as we simultaneously widened our baking repertoires, Americans found ways to streamline the process of baking in the interest of greater "convenience." As a result, it is now an easy matter to produce an excellent cake, using fresh ingredients and modern methods, without expending enormous amounts of time and effort.

What is the background that has led to cake baking as we know it today?

Many ancient sources mention cakes. These were primitive grain mixtures compared to the light products we know today, and were frequently heavily sweetened with honey. Over the years, cakes became identified with various religious and social ceremonies. This was true in widely varied cultures, and we still celebrate many ceremonies with traditional cakes. What is a birthday, for example, without a special cake, no matter how simple or elaborate?

The wedding cake is one of the best-known celebration cakes, but seldom has there been one so elaborate or so lovingly described as the one that was served to *Madame Bovary* on her wedding day: "... and when dessert time came he himself brought to the table a wedding cake that drew exclamations from all. Its base was a square of blue cardboard representing a temple with porticoes and colonnades and adorned on all sides with stucco statuettes standing in niches spangled with gold paper stars. The second tier was a mediaeval castle in *gâteau de Savoie*, surrounded by miniature fortifications of angelica, almonds, raisins, and orange sections. And finally, on the topmost layer—which was a green meadow, with rocks, jelly lakes, and boats of hazelnut shells—a little cupid was swinging in a chocolate swing. The tips of the two uprights, the highest points of the whole, were two real rosebuds." (Gustave Flaubert). Originally, the wedding cake seems to have been a honey cake, giving rise to the term honeymoon. Other less well-known holiday cakes include hot cross buns, eaten in England on Good Friday, and the simnel cake, an almond paste and currant-studded confection baked for the British equivalent of our Mother's Day.

Christmas has inspired home bakers throughout the world, and quite varied culinary cake traditions evolved over many generations. In Hungary, the traditional festive meal includes a roast suckling pig and poppy-seed cakes. In England, plum cakes were originally a symbol of the spices and fruits brought by the Three Kings.

In France, this celebration is called *reveillon,* and the best-known symbol of the holiday is a *bûche de Noël,* or yule log. This elegant cake consists of a rolled spongecake filled with buttercream, frosted with chocolate cream in a pattern that simulates the gnarled bark of a tree. It is garnished with meringue mushrooms, candied fruits, marzipan holly, and sugar "moss." This cake apparently is derived from an earlier Viking tradition, and it is seen in all parts of France and frequently in Italy. In Normandy, Christmas cakes are called *nourolles* or *aguigettes,* while in Brittany and Touraine, *fouaces,* or griddle cakes, are traditionally baked under the ashes in the hearth. These cakes were a favorite of Gargantua's in the novel by Rabelais.

The *Gâteau* (or *galette*) *des Rois* (kings' cake) is perhaps the favorite French holiday cake. This is served on January 6th, or Twelfth Night. A relic of a Roman pagan feast, custom dictates that a pea, bean, or coin is baked in the cake, and the person who finds the token in his piece of cake is the king or queen of the feast, blessed with good fortune. Some religious groups claimed that the good luck bean, called a *phoebe,* was a blasphemous pagan symbol, so it was sometimes replaced by a small china doll representing the Christ child. The *Gâteau des Rois,* shaped like a crown, takes sever-

al forms—a simple butter cake, a wafer, a rich puff pastry tart, or a sumptuous yeast-raised brioche with fruit.

English baking was more home-based than French, with the traditions of holidays and daily teatime calling for such English favorites as fruitcakes (also used for weddings), Dundee cake, jam roly-poly, and many others. The English have always preferred dense, rich fruitcakes, prompting one Englishman to describe the cakes as "black as the devil, heavy as sin, sweet as young love." Seedcake, flavored with caraway, was taken from England to America by early colonists.

In America, baking cakes in early ovens was not easy, but the pioneer spirit made homemade cakes popular wherever people settled. Cookbooks published before the Civil War, in fact, devoted more pages to recipes for cakes than for any other single item. Early favorites included seedcakes, Pennsylvania Dutch cakes baked with molasses, Austrian and European cakes with poppy seeds and ground nuts, angel-food cakes, and cakes baked with black walnuts. Election cakes, taken to rallies and meetings, were popular first in New England, then later the tradition was carried to the West.

Marble cake, baked by Mennonites in Virginia, first had a molasses batter as its dark component, rather than the chocolate batter we know today. An early recipe warned, "this cake will not keep unless it is put under lock and key." Other cakes popular in the early days of the South included coconut cake and Lady Baltimore cake, still popular today. This is an egg-white cake with a filling of pecans, figs, raisins and brandy, and frosted with a fluffy white frosting. Glenna McGinnis's Lane cake, served at holidays, was a similar concoction, frosted with a mixture of eggs, sugar, bourbon, pecans, coconut and raisins.

From the 1920s onward, baking cakes at home became considerably easier. For one thing, recipes were clearer and better written, offering more precise instructions which helped to prevent failures. Furthermore, measuring implements had become standardized, so that there was no guessing about "half a teacup of milk," or "butter the size of two eggs." Flour was being produced on a large scale, and several major companies featured new, carefully tested recipes in their advertising. The chiffon cake, for example, was first made with a new method developed in 1927 by Harry Baker, a California insurance salesman.

The one-bowl method of mixing cakes, with sifted dry ingredients being mixed directly into fat, flour, and liquid, was probably first introduced in about 1943. James Beard refers to a similar type of cake called "crazy cake." One big reason for the popularity of the one-bowl cake was that it produced good results with a minimum of time, effort and cleanup. The method has since been adapted to produce a variety of different cakes that can range anywhere from a simple, moist snacking cake to an elaborately filled layer cake suitable for further decoration.

With the advent of new labor-saving cake-making equipment and a growing concern about the freshness of ingredients, made-from-scratch cakes are very much back in vogue. In addition to the beloved old standbys such as pound cakes, devil's-food cake and other chocolate cakes, jelly rolls, upside-down cakes, angel-food cakes, and the 1–2–3–4 cake (named for the proportions of its principal ingredients), there is a whole batch of new cakes flavored with natural ingredients—carrots, nuts, honey, fresh citrus fruits and dried fruits.

Homemade cakes provide pleasure for family and friends, and for the cook as well. Michel Guérard, one of France's most respected chefs, says that he received much inspiration from his early days as an apprentice pastry cook: each day, the adolescent Guérard was required to create a new cake. Today, he is considered one of the most creative chefs in the world.

Whether based on favorite traditional recipes, or on updated ones using valid time-saving techniques such as the one-bowl mixing method, cakes are a worthwhile effort for the home baker—as long as they are freshly baked, with the best ingredients available. And today, still, cakes retain a goodly measure of symbolism and ceremony. When a homemade cake is served, it conveys a message of welcome, caring and celebration. Even a simple cake can transform an ordinary meal into a special occasion.

SIMPLE CAKES

Cakes made by the one-bowl method are simpler and quicker to make than other cakes. The one-bowl cake need recipes especially designed for the method. Do not use recipes designed for other procedures. The ingredients are easy to remember: equal weights of flour, sugar, fat and eggs, plus about 1⅓ teaspoons baking powder for each 1 cup (about 4 ounces) flour. Put all the ingredients in a large mixing bowl and beat them together until light and glossy.

If you are using self-rising flour, which already contains a certain amount of baking powder, you will not need to add additional leavening, as the amount in the flour is enough for these cakes.

Baking powder reacts with liquid and heat to produce a gas which expands, making the cake rise as it is baked. Baking powder begins to act as soon as it becomes damp, so be prepared to bake the cake as soon as it is mixed. (Store unused baking powder in an airtight container in a cool dry place.)

Soft or whipped margarine is perfect for this method. If you have only ordinary margarine or butter, let either soften in a warm room for at least 1 hour before using. The sugar also must be "soft." Use superfine white sugar, or soft brown sugar for a slightly richer, darker cake. Eggs must be at room temperature; remove from refrigerator 1 hour before you start to mix the batter. Use large eggs, 2 ounces each.

Using a pan of the correct size is essential for successful cake baking. If the pan is too small, the mixture can overflow, and you run the risk of a dome forming on the top of the cake and cracking, or the cake may sink in the middle because it is not cooked through. The depth is as important as the diameter: the same quantity of cake mixture will, for example, physically fit into one 8-inch deep round pan or two 9-inch shallow round pans. But the cooking time will be different. It is best to use the pan sizes specified in your recipe, but if you are forced to use an alternate size, be sure the substitute pan has the same volume capacity. A deeper pan requires additional cooking time, so simply adjust accordingly.

Use plain or nonstick pans, and grease all of them, whether nonstick or not. Ordinary pans must also be lined with wax paper or kitchen parchment or foil; cut the paper to fit the pan, and grease the top of the paper. Use melted margarine or butter or a flavorless oil to grease pans and paper; apply it with a pastry brush, making an even light coating.

Before you start to mix the cake batter, preheat the oven. By the time the oven has reached the correct temperature, in 15 minutes, your cake batter will be ready.

Fill a large mixing bowl with hot water so it will be at warm room temperature when you start. Prepare the cake pan (or pans), grease it and line it. If any ingredient needs preparing (melting, sieving, etc.), do that. Pour out the water in the mixing bowl and dry the bowl.

Stir the shortening before you add anything else to it, to be sure it is soft and creamy. Sift flour and baking powder into the warm bowl and add remaining ingredients. Or, for a better procedure, sift flour and baking powder into the bowl with the fat and add only part of the liquid. Beat vigorously for 2 minutes to make a fairly thick batter. Add eggs and remaining liquid and beat for 1 minute longer. Beat with a wooden spoon, using swift light movements, until the batter is glossy. Use full sweeping movements, cutting through the middle of the batter at intervals. If you use an electric mixer, you can time the beating by minutes. If you beat by hand, about 150 strokes equals 1 minute of mixing by machine. A food processor can be used for making cakes by the one-bowl method. Since the time required is only 60 seconds, one must be careful not to overprocess or cake will be tough. Follow the manufacturers instructions. Use a rubber or plastic spatula to scrape the batter into the prepared pan or pans, and smooth the top with the spatula.

Bake the cake for the time specified in the recipe; it will vary according to the size of the pan. Do not open the oven door until the whole time has elapsed as cold air can cause a cake to collapse. The cake is baked when it is well risen, firm to the touch, light golden in color. Test with a warm skewer; when you insert it into the center of the cake, it should come out clean, dry and hot.

Let the cake rest for 3 minutes after you remove it from the oven, then turn it out on a wire cake rack and let it cool. A large cake may need 3 hours to cool completely, layers about 1 hour.

Cake batter made by the one-bowl method is ideal for making cupcakes or other small cakes. Spoon the prepared batter into paper baking cups or greased cupcake pans. Bake in a preheated 350°F oven for 20 minutes, until golden brown. Test with a skewer to be sure that the cupcakes are done. Turn them out onto a rack to cool. When completely cooled, frost and decorate tops as desired.

Cake Variations

A basic one-bowl cake offers a wide range of flavor, filling and icing variations.

Here are some ideas for flavoring cake and icing.
• For lemon cake, add lemon juice and grated rind to the basic recipe.
• For orange cake, use orange liqueur, orange food coloring, and some finely grated orange rind.
• For a golden color, use butter instead of margarine.
• For coffee flavoring, use coffee essence or instant coffee powder dis-

Preparing a Layer Cake Pan

1 Place cake pan on lining paper and outline the size of the base.

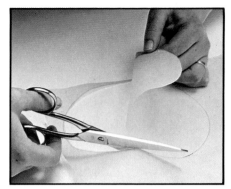

2 Cut out the circle of paper, just inside the penciled outline.

3 Place the paper round in a greased pan, then grease the paper and sides of pan.

Preparing a Deep Pan

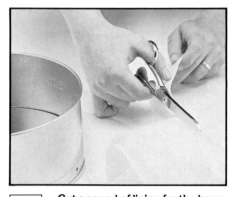

1 Cut a round of lining for the base. Cut a strip to go around the edges, 2½ inches deeper than the pan with a 1-inch overlap.

2 Fold over ½ inch on a long side of strip and crease firmly. Snip the folded edge diagonally at ½-inch intervals.

3 Grease sides and base of pan. Place strip with snipped edge on base and the round in pan. Fully grease lining.

Preparing a Ring Pan

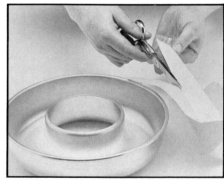

1 Cut 15 to 20 strips of lining paper into 1-inch by 7-inch pieces. Grease pan.

2 Push the strips into the pan so they lie across the tunnel.

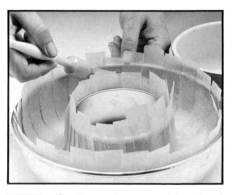

3 Overlap strips around inside of pan. Grease thoroughly.

One-Bowl Cake

One 9-inch layer cake

1 cup cake flour and 1⅓
  teaspoons baking
  powder
  or 1 cup self-rising cake
  flour
½ cup superfine granulated
  sugar
4 ounces unsalted butter or
  margarine, at room
  temperature
2 large eggs
½ teaspoon vanilla extract or
  other desired flavoring

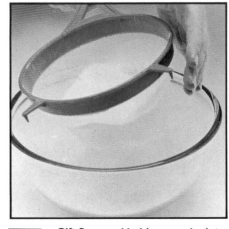

1 Sift flour and baking powder into a warmed large mixing bowl.

2 Add sugar, soft fat, eggs and any flavoring. Beat for 2 to 3 minutes, until batter is glossy.

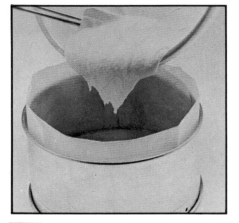

3 With a spatula scrape the batter into the prepared pan.

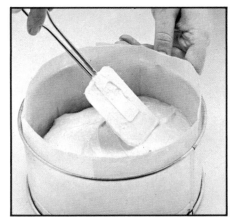

4 Smooth the top with a spatula. Bake a cake at 325°F, cupcakes at 350°F.

5 Test the cake with a warmed cake skewer. It should come out clean, dry and hot.

6 Let the baked cake rest for 3 minutes to shrink a little from the sides of the pan.

7 Place a wire rack on top of cake pan and carefully invert rack and pan together.

8 Gently remove cake pan. Peel off the lining paper and leave cake until completely cool.

solved in milk or water. Regular prepared coffee will not give enough flavor.

• For a chocolate cake use powdered cocoa and soft brown sugar instead of white sugar.

• Add a few chocolate chips to the batter for a polka-dot cake.

• Use thick preserves for jam filling in a layer cake.

• Mix cream cheese with thick cream for a smooth filling.

• For chocolate butter icing, sift powdered cocoa with the sugar, or add melted chocolate to the butter.

Layer cakes can be sandwiched together with jam, honey or marmalade, lemon curd or fruit purée, soft cheese mixed with chopped fruit, mashed banana mixed with brown sugar and lemon juice, melted chocolate and butter, whipped cream mixed with fruit or flavored with a liqueur. Try to match the filling and icing. Some cakes are sandwiched together with part of the icing.

For decorations, one can go from simple to complex. The easiest, of course, are the uncooked icings and glazes. Cooked frostings such as meringue frostings, are slightly more complicated, in that the use of a sugar thermometer is essential.

Simple Sugar Decorations. A simple but elegant topping can be arranged by placing a doily on the cake and sifting powdered sugar onto the cake through the doily. Carefully lift off the doily to reveal the lacy pattern.

Confectioners' Sugar Icing. This is simply confectioners' sugar mixed with water, milk, fruit juice, coffee, liqueur. Sift 1 cup sugar into a bowl and mix with 1 to 2 tablespoons liquid. For a softer icing that will drip down the sides of the cake, add a little more liquid, teaspoon by teaspoon.

Butter Icing. Sift 1 cup confectioners' sugar into a bowl; let 4 tablespoons butter soften at room temperature. Beat together until butter is creamed and sugar completely dissolved in the butter. Flavor with 1 ounce melted unsweetened chocolate, 1 tablespoon unsweetened powdered cocoa, 2 teaspoons coffee essence or instant coffee powder, ½ teaspoon vanilla extract or other flavoring extract, finely grated rind and juice of ½ orange or lemon; ½ ounce chopped nuts.

When the cake is cool, carefully trim it to be sure it is symmetrical in shape; often there will be a little shrinking or falling in baking. Cut off any very crisp edges. Brush off all loose crumbs. For an extra flourish, melt a few tablespoons of jelly and brush it on top and sides of cake to keep any remaining crumbs from sticking up and spoiling the icing. Scoop or pour icing onto the cake and gently spread it evenly with a spatula.

When you cut a cake, use a very sharp knife or a "cake-breaker," a utensil like a large comb which will separate the cake without mashing it. If you use a knife, insert the point into the center and gently pull it toward you with a short sawing motion.

Storage and Freezing

Plain cakes, not frosted or decorated, can be stored in an airtight container in a cool place for 3 days. Frosted or decorated cakes need to be stored in the refrigerator. Cakes can be frozen and will keep for 6 months. If they are decorated, let them freeze solid before wrapping them, to keep the decorations from being damaged; then wrap in airtight containers. If you are freezing plain layers, they can be stacked, but be sure to separate them with sheets of wax paper or freezer paper. Be sure to store a cake in the kind of container that has a flat base with a domed lid; cakes do not get damaged in these.

Traditionally even stale cakes, several days old, are never thrown out. Individual slices can be doused with a flavored liqueur and topped with whipped cream.

Slicing a Deep Cake Into Halves

1 Place cake on a board and set board at eye level. Use a large knife with serrated edge.

2 Insert knife tip into the center of the cake. Holding the knife straight and steady, turn the cake around until it is sliced.

3 Separate the halves and place bottom half, cut side down, on a cake plate. Spread with filling. Set top half in place.

Confectioners' Sugar Icing

1   cup sugar
1   to 2 tablespoons liquid

    Butter Icing

1   cup sugar
2   ounces unsalted butter
½   ounce chopped nuts, or ½
        teaspoon vanilla extract,
        or other flavoring

1 *Simple Sugar Decorations:* Place a lace doily on top of the cake. Sift confectioners' sugar onto the cake through the doily.

2 Gently lift off the doily. Use fingertips so that the lacy pattern is not smudged.

1 *Butter Icing:* Cream butter with a wooden spoon.

2 Sift in confectioners' sugar and flavoring. Beat until sugar is completely dissolved and the icing is creamy.

1 *Confectioners' Sugar Icing:* Sift confectioners' sugar through a fine sieve into a bowl.

2 Beat in the warm liquid (water, fruit juice, liqueur, etc.) and any flavoring and coloring.

3 Beat vigorously for 3 minutes, until sugar is completely dissolved and icing shiny and smooth.

4 Pour icing onto cake and spread evenly with a metal spatula.

Meringue Frosting

enough frosting for an
8-inch cake

1	cup plus 2 tablespoons granulated sugar
¼	cup water
	pinch of cream of tartar
1	large egg white
	pinch of salt
½	teaspoon vanilla extract

• As a cake frosting, this meringue has a shiny surface and a marshmallow texture.

• A sugar thermometer is essential for the successful preparation of the syrup.

• The frosting must be spread on the cake as soon as it is ready, or it will begin to harden.

• The meringue can be tinted with food coloring; add it at the same time as the flavoring. Colored frosting is good for cakes for children's parties.

1 Put sugar and water in a heavy pan over low heat. Stir until sugar is dissolved. Stir in cream of tartar.

2 Bring syrup to a boil and cook without stirring to 248°F on the sugar thermometer. Brush down sides of pan with a wet brush.

3 Meanwhile, beat egg white and salt until stiff. Remove syrup from heat and let the bubbles subside.

4 Beating constantly, pour the hot, not boiling, syrup onto the beaten egg white.

5 Add vanilla or other flavoring. Beat at high speed until frosting thickens, turns opaque, will coat a spoon, and is almost cold.

6 Additions such as grated citrus rinds, chopped nuts or raisins should be made at the last moment, before spreading the cake.

7 Working quickly, pour meringue onto cake and spread with a wet, warm spatula. Add any decorations before frosting sets.

Maple Syrup Icing

enough frosting for an
8-inch cake

2   large egg whites
3   tablespoons maple syrup

As no sugar boiling is necessary, this soft, light icing is easy to make. Maple syrup is most delicious, but other syrups can be substituted.

1 Place egg whites and syrup in the top pan of a double boiler, but do not yet place over heat.

2 Beat whites and syrup together, then place top pan over simmering water in the lower pan.

Dundee Cake (Scottish Fruitcake)

Dundee cake is one of the traditional Scottish fruitcakes. It is elegantly and simply decorated with almond halves. This cake is also used often as a wedding cake, stacked in tiered layers with lots of snow-white icing.

• To chop candied fruits easily, first coat the blade of a chef's knife with a little flavorless vegetable oil or almond oil. Or use kitchen scissors, and coat the blades with oil.

• Whole candied fruits and already chopped fruits are available. Choose those already chopped to simplify the preparation.

• Blanched almonds are easy to split; just separate along the natural division.

• If this cake is tightly wrapped, it will keep for 2 weeks or longer. It will improve with age if you wrap it first in a piece of cheesecloth that has been soaked in brandy, sherry or Madeira. If it becomes dry, soak it with more of the spirit or wine.

8 to 10 portions

¼   cup candied citrus peel or citron
¼   cup glacé cherries
4   ounces blanched almonds
½   cup dried currants
½   cup dark raisins
½   cup light raisins

10   ounces unsalted butter
1   cup light brown sugar
2½   cups all-purpose flour
½   teaspoon ground cinnamon
½   teaspoon ground allspice
½   teaspoon ground ginger
1   teaspoon grated lemon rind
4   large eggs

1 Line an 8-inch round cake pan with parchment or wax paper. Tie a double thickness of brown paper around the outside of the pan.

2 Preheat oven to 325°F. Cut up the candied peel or citron with scissors or knife, oiled to prevent sticking.

Dundee Cake (continued)

Dundee Cake (continued)

3 Wash syrup from the cherries with warm water. Pat dry. With a sharp knife cut the cherries into halves.

4 Chop 2 ounces of the almonds. Split the other 2 ounces lengthwise. Toss fruit and chopped nuts with a little flour.

5 Cream butter and brown sugar with a wooden spoon or an electric mixer until light and fluffy.

6 Sift flour with the spices. Add lemon rind to the creamed butter. Beat eggs, add a little of the egg to creamed butter mixture.

7 Add egg and flour alternately until all have been added. Stir in all the fruits and the chopped almonds.

8 Spoon the mixture into the prepared pan. Smooth the top, then make a hollow in the center to prevent peaking during baking.

9 Arrange the halved almonds on top in concentric circles. Put a thick piece of newspaper on a baking sheet and set the cake pan on the newspaper.

10 Bake for 2½ to 3 hours. When top becomes brown, cover it with foil. At end of baking time, test with a skewer; if not done, bake for a few minutes longer.

11 Cool the cake in the pan, then turn onto a wire cooling rack. Cool completely before wrapping or storing.

Strawberry Charlotte Malakoff

Strawberry Charlotte Malakoff (continued)

10 portions

40	ladyfingers, approximately
5	cups strawberries
¼	pound unsalted butter, softened
⅓	cup granulated sugar
5	tablespoons Grand Marnier liqueur
3	ounces blanched almonds
⅔	cup heavy cream
1	cup whipped cream, slightly sweetened

This elegant charlotte, filled with delicious strawberries, looks difficult, but it is actually assembled with a series of easy techniques.

• Ladyfingers may be purchased or made at home.

• Use a food processor or nut grinder to grind the almonds. Once they are ground, mix in a little of the creamed butter to give a creamy texture.

• Charlotte fillings can be chocolate or other mousse, fruit-studded whipped cream, ice cream, gelatin-stabilized custards such as Bavarian cream, fresh or dried fruits.

• If you do not have a charlotte mold, use a 6-cup soufflé dish or a straight-sided casserole.

• After filling the mold, trim the tops of the ladyfingers flush with the top of the mold, or, if the mold is not filled to the top, cut them off even with the top of the filling.

• Charlottes are firm enough to be unmolded, so they are a good choice for a buffet.

1 Choose a 1½-quart metal charlotte mold, at least 4 inches deep. Or choose a soufflé dish (pictures 5, 9, 10).

2 Lay ladyfingers round side down and cut one end to a point, preparing enough to fill the base of the mold.

6 Cream butter and sugar together until light and fluffy. Beat in the Grand Marnier, a little at a time.

7 Grind the almonds in a food processor or nut grinder. Beat into the butter mixture. Whip ⅔ cup cream until stiff.

11 Continue layering until the cream is used, ending with a layer of ladyfingers. Cover with a plate and weight it.

12 Chill 3 to 5 hours. Run knife around the mold, place plate on top, and invert. Lift off mold and lining.

3 Fit the ladyfingers in place to be sure the fit is exact. Remove them temporarily.

4 Brush the base and sides of the mold with flavorless oil. Line the base with wax paper, and replace the cut ladyfingers.

5 Arrange more ladyfingers, round side out, against the sides of the mold, fitting them close together with no space between.

8 Fold almond and butter mixture into the cream and spoon one third of it into the bottom of the mold.

9 Wash, dry and hull strawberries. Cut into halves, reserving 1 cup for garnish. Cover almond cream with a layer of berries.

10 Cover strawberries with a layer of ladyfingers, cut to fit in the same fashion as the layer in the bottom.

13 Garnish top of the charlotte with some of the reserved strawberries.

14 Pipe sweetened whipped cream around the base of the charlotte; use a pastry bag and make pretty mounds.

15 Insert strawberry slices between the mounds of cream. Serve as soon as decorated, or the cake will get soggy.

Poppy-Seed Cake

One 9-inch tube cake

1 cup poppy seeds
⅓ cup honey
¼ cup water
8 ounces butter or
    shortening
1½ cups sugar
4 eggs, separated
1 teaspoon vanilla extract

1 cup dairy sour cream
2½ cups sifted all-purpose
    flour
1 teaspoon baking soda
1 teaspoon salt
Vanilla Frosting (recipe
    follows)
poppy seeds for garnish

Preheat oven to 350°F. Butter and lightly flour a 9-inch tube pan. Cook poppy seeds with the honey and water in a small saucepan for 5 to 7 minutes. Cool.

Cream butter and sugar until light and fluffy. Add poppy-seed mixture, then the egg yolks, one at a time, beating well after each addition. Blend in vanilla and sour cream. Sift dry ingredients together, and add a little at a time to the poppy-seed mixture, beating well each time. Beat egg whites until stiff and fold into the batter. Pour or spoon into the prepared pan.

Bake the cake for 1 hour and 15 to 20 minutes, until cake tests done. Cool in the pan for 5 minutes, then remove from the pan and cool on a wire rack. Frost with vanilla frosting and sprinkle additional poppy seeds over the top.

Vanilla Frosting

2 tablespoons butter or
    margarine
1¾ cups sifted confectioners'
    sugar

2 tablespoons milk
    pinch of salt
¾ teaspoon vanilla extract

Cream butter until soft and fluffy. Add confectioners' sugar alternately with the milk until mixture is of spreading consistency. Blend in salt and vanilla. Spread frosting over the top of the cake, and let some of it dribble down the sides.

Devil's-Food Cake

One 9-inch layer cake

2½ cups all-purpose flour
2 teaspoons baking soda
    pinch of salt
4 ounces unsalted butter or
    margarine
1 cup plus 2 tablespoons
    firmly packed light brown
    sugar

2 large eggs
4 ounces unsweetened
    chocolate
⅞ cup dairy sour cream
    Butter-Sugar Filling (recipe
    follows)
    Chocolate Butter Frosting
    (recipe follows)

Preheat oven to 350°F. Butter two 9-inch layer-cake pans, line with paper, and butter the paper. Sift flour, baking soda and salt together and set aside.

In a large bowl, cream butter and sugar together until fluffy. Add eggs, one at a time, beating well after each addition. Place the chocolate in a bowl set over hot water and let it melt. Beat the melted chocolate into the creamed mixture. Beat a little of the flour into the mixture, then continue adding the dry ingredients alternately with the sour cream until all is incorporated. Spoon the batter into the prepared pans.

Bake for 40 minutes, until cakes are firm to the touch. Cool on a wire rack. Spread the butter-sugar filling on one layer and place the second on top. Spread the frosting over the top and sides in swirls. Let the cake wait for 1 day before slicing and serving it.

Butter-Sugar Filling

3	ounces unsalted butter	1	tablespoon light cream
1	cup confectioners' sugar, sifted		

Cream the butter until soft and fluffy. Beat in the sifted sugar and the cream alternately, adding a little of each at a time, until it is all incorporated and the filling is smooth.

Chocolate Butter Frosting

6	ounces chocolate chips	2	large egg yolks
3	ounces unsalted butter	1	pound confectioners' sugar

Melt chocolate chips and butter in a bowl set over hot water. Let chocolate cool slightly. Beat egg yolks and stir into the chocolate and butter. Add confectioners' sugar, 1 tablespoon at a time. Beat the mixture smooth after each addition. As the mixture stiffens, beat in 2 tablespoons hot water. Continue beating until all the sugar is incorporated.

All-in-One Chocolate Cake

One 8-inch layer cake

1½ cups cake flour
1½ teaspoons baking powder
6 ounces unsalted butter or
    margarine, softened
¾ cup firmly packed light
    brown sugar

3 large eggs
2½ tablespoons powdered
    cocoa
2½ tablespoons boiling water
    Chocolate Cream Frosting
    (recipe follows)
    blanched almonds

Preheat oven to 325°F. Butter two 8-inch round cake pans, each 1½ inches deep. Line the bottom of both pans with wax paper and butter the paper.

Sift flour and baking powder into a large bowl. Add butter or margarine, brown sugar and eggs. Blend powdered cocoa with boiling water and stir into the mixture. Beat with a hand-held electric mixer, or with a wooden spoon for 2 minutes, until well blended. Divide the batter equally between the 2 pans and smooth the surface.

Bake the cakes for 25 to 30 minutes, until springy to the touch. Cool cakes for 2 minutes, then turn them out of the pans and peel off the lining papers. Turn the cakes right side up and let them cool completely.

Use half of the frosting, which will be soft, to sandwich the layers together. Spread remaining frosting on top. Just before serving, decorate the top of the cake with blanched almonds.

Chocolate Cream Frosting

5 ounces semisweet
    chocolate
1 ounce white vegetable
    shortening

2 tablespoons maple syrup
6 tablespoons light cream

Break the chocolate into pieces and put into a heatproof bowl with the shortening. Set the bowl over a pan of barely simmering water and let it remain until the chocolate is melted; stir occasionally. Remove the bowl from the hot water and stir in the syrup and cream. Cover and set aside to cool; frosting will thicken as it cools.

Variation: Omit the almonds for garnish. Cut cake into slices and freeze, then pack into a rigid container with wax paper separating the slices. Store in the freezer for up to 2 months. Defrost unwrapped at room temperature for 1 to 1½ hours.

Cornish Seedcake

One 9-inch tube cake

8 ounces unsalted butter
1 cup sugar
4 large eggs
2 cups all-purpose flour

2 teaspoons baking powder
½ teaspoon salt
2½ tablespoons caraway seeds
2 to 4 tablespoons milk

Preheat oven to 350°F. Butter and flour a 9-inch tube pan. In a large bowl cream the butter; add sugar, and cream until sugar is no longer grainy. Add the eggs, one at a time, beating well after each addition. Sift flour, baking powder and salt together and add little by little to the creamed mixture. Finally stir in the caraway seeds. Add enough of the milk to make a batter that is moist but still rather stiff. Beat the mixture by hand for about 4 minutes or with an electric mixer at medium speed for 1 minute. Pour or spoon batter into the prepared pan.

Bake the cake for 50 minutes, or until a cake tester comes out hot and dry. Let the cake rest in the pan for 10 minutes, then turn it out and cool on a wire rack.

Gâteau au Citron

(French Lemon Cake)

Processor Method

One 8-inch round cake

1 large lemon	1 cup less 2 tablespoons all-purpose flour
1½ cups granulated sugar	2 tablespoons cornstarch
4 ounces unsalted butter	1 teaspoon baking powder
2 large eggs	1 cup confectioners' sugar

Preheat oven to 325°F. Adjust rack to center position. Butter and flour an 8-inch round cake pan. With a vegetable peeler, remove the lemon rind and cut it into 2-inch pieces. Extract the juice and set aside for the glaze.

Insert metal blade in the bowl of a food processor; add the pieces of lemon rind and the granulated sugar. Process until rind is grated, about 60 seconds. Cut butter into 8 pieces and add to the lemon rind; process until smooth, about another 30 seconds. Add eggs and process for about 30 seconds again. Scrape down sides of bowl as needed.

Sift flour, cornstarch and baking powder together. Add dry ingredients to processor bowl and turn machine on and off quickly, just until flour is absorbed. Do not overprocess at

this stage or the cake will be tough instead of soft and tender. Transfer batter to the prepared pan.

Bake for about 25 minutes, or until a toothpick inserted in the center of the cake comes out dry and very warm. Cool cake slightly in the pan, then remove from pan and place on a wire rack over a sheet of wax paper.

Mix confectioners' sugar and the reserved lemon juice until smooth (add a few more drops of lemon juice or more sugar if necessary to make the glaze suitable for spooning). Spoon some of the glaze over the top of the cake. As cake cools, continue to spoon on the glaze, until it is all used. When cake is completely cold, wrap in plastic wrap and refrigerate.

Variation: Substitute lime rind and juice for lemon.

Gingerbread Squares

9 large squares

1½	cups cake flour	½	teaspoon ground cinnamon
1	teaspoon baking powder	½	teaspoon grated nutmeg
½	teaspoon baking soda	2	ounces unsalted butter
⅓	cup sugar	½	cup water
1	teaspoon ground ginger	½	cup molasses

Preheat oven to 325°F. Butter an 8- or 9-inch square pan; line the bottom with buttered wax paper.

Sift all dry ingredients into the large bowl of an electric mixer; stir to blend. Combine butter, water and molasses in a small saucepan; bring to a boil, stirring constantly. Pour the hot mixture over the flour mixture and beat for 30 seconds, or just until batter is smooth. Pour batter into the prepared pan.

Bake gingerbread for 30 to 35 minutes, until a toothpick inserted in the center comes out hot and dry. Cool the cake in the pan for 3 minutes before turning it out on a wire rack.

Cut cake into squares; serve warm or cold. To serve *à la mode,* top with lemon sauce, applesauce, fresh fruit, whipped cream or ice cream.

Applesauce Spice Cakes

**36 small cupcakes or 1 sheet
cake, 13 × 9 inches**

3	cups cake flour	6	ounces unsalted butter, at room temperature
2½	teaspoons baking powder		
1	cup superfine granulated sugar	2	large eggs
		1	cup applesauce
2	teaspoons ground cinnamon	½	cup dark seedless raisins
		2	tart red apples
			lemon juice

Preheat oven to 350°F. Sift flour, baking powder, sugar and cinnamon into the large bowl of an electric mixer. Add butter, eggs and applesauce. Beat at medium speed until well mixed. Stir in the raisins. Divide batter among 36 fluted paper baking cups or lightly greased muffin pans. Bake for 20 to 25 minutes, until cakes test done.

Or pour batter into a prepared sheet pan, 13 × 9 × 2 inches, and bake in the preheated oven for 30 to 35 minutes.

Cool cupcakes or sheet cake on a wire rack.

At serving time, prepare the apple garnish. Core apples and cut into thin slices or wedges. Dip the pieces into lemon juice to prevent browning. Garnish each cupcake or slice of cake with an apple slice.

Variations: Substitute 1 cup banana, apricot, raspberry or plum purée for the applesauce. Substitute diced dried fruit, chopped nuts or chocolate chips for the raisins.

English Cider Cake

One deep 9-inch cake

4	ounces unsalted butter	1½	teaspoons baking powder
½	cup granulated sugar	1	teaspoon grated nutmeg
2	large eggs	¾	cup apple cider (see note)
1¾	cups all-purpose flour	¼	cup dried currants
¼	cup cornstarch		

Preheat oven to 350°F. Butter and flour a deep 9-inch cake pan. Cream the butter, then beat in the sugar until it is no longer grainy. Add the eggs, one at a time, beating well after each addition. Sift flour, cornstarch, baking powder and nutmeg together. Stir half of the dry ingredients into the creamed mixture, then pour in the cider; beat thoroughly. Add remaining flour mixture and again beat thoroughly. Then beat in the currants. Pour the batter into the prepared pan.

Bake the cake for 45 minutes. Let it cool in the pan for 10 minutes, then turn out and cool completely. If you like, spread the cake with confectioners' sugar icing made with apple brandy as the liquid.

Note: English cider is fizzy and slightly alcoholic. If you wish to have a taste closer to the original country cake, substitute 1 tablespoon apple brandy and 2 tablespoons ginger ale for 3 tablespoons of the cider.

Madeira Cake

One deep 7-inch cake

*There is no Madeira in this cake, but it is
the perfect accompaniment to that delicate
wine and is also good with tea.*

2 cups all-purpose flour	4 large eggs
2 teaspoons baking powder	2 to 3 tablespoons milk
pinch of salt	(optional)
6 ounces unsalted butter	2 thin slices of candied citron
¾ cup superfine granulated sugar	

Preheat oven to 350°F. Adjust rack to center position. Butter and fully line a deep 7-inch round cake pan.

Sift flour, baking powder and salt into a medium-size bowl. Place butter in a large bowl and beat with a wooden spoon until soft and light. Add the sugar, and cream the ingredients together until light and fluffy. Stop beating occasionally to scrape down sides of the bowl with a spatula. Whisk the eggs together and add gradually to the creamed mixture, beating after each addition. If any sign of curdling occurs, add a little of the sifted flour. When all the eggs have been incorporated, scrape down the spoon and bowl and beat again for 1 minute. Gently fold in the sifted dry ingredients until completely mixed in. If necessary, add enough of the milk to give the batter a soft dropping consistency. Spoon the batter into the prepared pan and smooth the surface with a spatula.

Bake the cake for 30 minutes, then without removing the pan from the oven, carefully lay the citron across the center of the cake. Close the oven door and bake for 1¼ hours longer. Let the cake cool in the pan for 10 minutes before turning it out. Cool it completely.

Variations: To make a ginger cake, omit citron; sift ½ teaspoon ground ginger with the flour; add 4 ounces preserved gingerroot, rinsed, drained, dried, and chopped, when all the flour has been folded into the batter. To make a coconut cake, omit citron; add 4 ounces flaked coconut to the sifted flour.

Apricot Fruitcake

One loaf cake

2 cups cake flour	3 eggs
2 teaspoons baking powder	1 cup dried apricot halves
6 ounces unsalted butter, at room temperature	1 cup candied cherries
1½ cups firmly packed light brown sugar	1⅓ cups dark seedless raisins

Preheat oven to 325°F. Butter a loaf pan, 9 × 5 × 3 inches, and line the bottom with buttered wax paper.

Place flour, baking powder, sugar and eggs in the large bowl of an electric mixer. Beat at medium speed for 1 minute, or until ingredients are just blended. With scissors cut apricots and cherries into small pieces. Stir these fruits and the raisins into the batter. Spoon the batter into the prepared pan.

Bake for 1 hour, or until a toothpick inserted in the center of the loaf comes out hot and with no batter sticking to it (it may not be dry because the fruits are moist). Cool cake in the pan for 10 minutes, then turn out on a wire rack.

The finished cake may be flavored with rum or brandy. Pierce the cake all over with a thin skewer, and sprinkle with 2 ounces of the spirit. Wrap in liquor-soaked cheesecloth, then in plastic wrap. Store cake for at least 1 day before serving it, to allow the flavors to blend.

Variation: Vary the fruits or substitute some chopped nuts or chocolate chips, as long as the total quantity of fruit mixture is 3⅓ cups.

Walnut Layer Cake

One 6-inch layer cake or one loaf cake

1½ cups all-purpose flour	¾ cup firmly packed soft brown sugar
1 teaspoon baking powder	2 teaspoons coffee essence
pinch of salt	3 large eggs
6 ounces unsalted butter or margarine	3 ounces shelled walnuts
	2 tablespoons milk (optional)

Frosting

1 large egg white	2 tablespoons cold water
6 ounces superfine granulated sugar	pinch of cream of tartar

Preheat oven to 350°F. Adjust rack to center position. Butter a deep 6-inch cake pan or a loaf pan, 9 × 5 × 3 inches. Line the pan completely and butter the lining paper.

Sift flour, baking powder and salt together into a bowl; set aside. In a large bowl, cream the butter until soft and light. Add sugar, and cream ingredients together until light and fluffy. Scrape down the spoon and sides of the bowl with a spatula. Add coffee essence, a little at a time, beating well. Whisk the eggs lightly, then add gradually to the creamed mixture, beating well after each addition. If any signs of curdling occur, add a little of the sifted flour. Scrape down the spoon and sides of the bowl again, and beat for 1 minute.

Set aside 8 perfect walnut halves; chop remaining nuts to small pieces, no larger than a lentil. Gently fold the sifted dry ingredients into the creamed mixture until completely incorporated. Fold in chopped walnuts. If necessary, add enough of the milk to give a soft dropping consistency. Spoon mixture into the prepared pan and smooth the top with a spatula.

Bake the cake for 1 to 1¼ hours, until well risen and evenly browned. Let the cake cool in the pan for 5 minutes before turning it out, then cool it completely on a wire rack. Cut the cooled cake horizontally into 3 equal layers. Set the bottom layer on a wire rack over a sheet of wax paper.

Make the frosting: Put all the frosting ingredients in a large bowl and beat together with a rotary egg beater or with a hand-held electric mixer, until mixed together. Set the bowl over a pan of hot, not boiling, water. Beat for 7 to 10 minutes if using an egg beater, for 2 to 3 minutes if using an electric mixer, until the frosting stands in soft peaks.

Spread a scant quarter of the frosting on the bottom layer. Set middle layer in place and spread another scant quarter of frosting on top. Set remaining cake layer in place. Using a small palette knife, quickly spread remaining frosting on top of the cake and down the sides. Swirl frosting decoratively. Place the reserved 8 walnut halves around the edge of the cake. Serve this cake the day you decorate it.

Note: To make coffee essence, dissolve 2 teaspoons instant coffee powder in 2 teaspoons water.

Pineapple Upside-Down Cake

One 9-inch square cake

5 ounces unsalted butter	2 teaspoons baking powder
1/3 cup firmly packed dark brown sugar	1 cup superfine granulated sugar
2 cups crushed pineapple, drained	1/2 cup milk
2 cups cake flour	2 large eggs
	1 teaspoon almond extract

Preheat oven to 350°F. Put 1 ounce of the butter in a deep 9-inch-square pan and melt the butter on top of the stove over medium heat. Add the brown sugar and stir until sugar is dissolved in the butter. Add pineapple and stir until the mixture is hot. Set the pan aside in a warm place.

Sift flour, baking powder and superfine sugar into the large bowl of an electric mixer. Add remaining 4 ounces butter, the milk, eggs and almond extract. Beat at medium speed for 2 minutes, until batter is well blended. Spoon batter over the pineapple mixture and smooth the top. Bake for 35 to 40 minutes, until a cake tester inserted in the center of the cake comes out hot and dry.

As soon as the cake is removed from the oven, invert the pan on a serving plate. Let the pan remain over the cake for about 1 minute, to allow the topping to settle on the cake. Lift off the pan. Serve the cake warm or cool, with sweetened whipped cream, if desired.

Part Five

AUTUMN ENTERTAINING

Harvest: the very word suggests plenty. What better way to enjoy the season's bounty than to share it with good friends? An Indian summer evening may offer one last chance to grill outdoors, or perhaps the crisp air will bring the party indoors before a crackling fire. Whatever the weather, an early autumn dinner is a lovely way to welcome friends back from vacations and to anticipate the holiday season ahead.

This is the time when robust appetites, jaded by summer sorbets and salads, need perking up with sizzling appetizers or soups: oysters, mushrooms or chicken livers wrapped in bacon, hot and peppery; scented, perhaps, with 1 sage leaf or a sprig of thyme; hearty homemade soups made with ripe garden vegetables and seasoned with herbs. Marinated meats are wonderful cooked on the grill, or, if the weather turns too chilly for outdoor cookery, broiled in the oven. The marinade has a two-fold purpose: it seasons the meat to make it tastier and bring out its natural juiciness, and it breaks down the fibers of the meat, making it fork-tender.

Hearty salads are very much at home with broiled meats, and a salad containing vegetables, cooked dried beans and salad greens is a port-manteau accompaniment that serves as vegetable, starch and salad for the meal. A well-seasoned herb bread, dripping with butter or olive oil, would be a welcome companion to this simple yet stylish food.

Autumn desserts? Fruits of the season—apples, pears, plums, and whatever else is seasonal in your area, perhaps baked into a luscious cake.

For the hostess who enjoys setting a pretty table, a harvest dinner is the time for colorful table appointments: brilliant blue, yellow, or orange tablecloth and napkins make for a warm and friendly atmosphere. Napkins can be folded to form a pocket to hold one perfect chrysanthemum, or a last orange marigold.

Centerpieces at this time of year can be lavish and almost outrageous: A bountiful mass of tiny pumpkins, autumn leaves, winter squash, red and green peppers spilling down the center of the table; a pyramid of apples, grapes and turban squash cascading from a basket and making a great conversation piece. Or you might opt for a monochromatic arrangement: On a royal blue cloth arrange purple plums, eggplant, grapes and lavendar Michaelmas daisies; or feature a family of greens with Savoy cabbage, green grapes, greengage plums, bunches of green herbs and a mat of asparagus fronds.

The colors of your harvest place settings can be echoed in the garnishing of the food: pickled green cherry tomatoes for the appetizers, herb-scented croutons and green-pepper slices for the soup; paper-thin slices of sweet onion and a dusting of parsley for the meat; whatever in your garden or farm stand looks appetizing and suitable. Carrot tops are edible and interesting garnishes. People eat with their eyes as well as savor with their taste buds, so you will want to make the food look, as well as taste, mouth-watering.

As you will see in the dinner plan, much can be made ahead, so try to save the day of the party for prettying up the house and dining table. And do leave yourself time for a bath and relaxation before your guests arrive. If you enjoy your own party, you can be certain your guests will as well.

SIMPLE HARVEST DINNER FOR EIGHT

Angels on Horseback
Fresh Tomato Soup with Herb Croutons
Red Pepper, Chick-pea and
Romaine Salad
Broiled Flank Steak with Dry Marinade
Garlic Herb Bread
Country Apple Cake and Vanilla Ice Cream
Wine Suggestion:
California Zinfandel

Zinfandel

Red, full bodied and robust, with an alcohol content of 11½ to 14½ %, California Zinfandel is probably more akin to the Bordeaux, or Claret, wines, than the Burgundies, and is an excellent choice for barbecues, marinated meats, game, and other strongly flavored and spicy foods.

Taylor California Cellars makes a very nice Zinfandel as does Paul Masson. Some small wineries that also produce a lovely Zinfandel: Ridge, Sutterhome, San Martin, Bandiera, John B. Merritt. The best Zinfandels generally come from Amador County in California, and there is even a white Zinfandel available.

If Zinfandel isn't your choice, any hearty red wine will go excellently with the Harvest Dinner. A California jug wine, served in an elegant decanter or pitcher and slightly chilled, will still earn you top marks as a good host. And with today's emphasis on white wines, a decanter of Chablis as an alternative selection is a thoughtful addition to the dinner table.

MARKET LIST

Meat and Fish

Oysters (2 dozen)
Meaty bacon (16 slices)
Flank steak (4 to 5 pounds)

Fruits and Vegetables

Romaine lettuce (1 large)
Red peppers (1 large)
Chick peas (4 cups)
Onions (3 large)
Tomatoes (8 large)
Parsley (2 bunches)
Basil (2 bunches)
Garlic (1 head)
Apples for cooking (10)

Staples

Paprika
Toothpicks
Vegetable oil
Ketchup
Flour
Chicken stock
**Bread—sliced bread and
 unsliced French bread**
Butter
Eggs
Salt
Sugar
Black pepper
Dijon-style mustard
Heavy cream
Wine vinegar
Garlic powder
Orégano
Baking soda
Cinnamon
Walnuts
Vanilla extract
Vanilla ice cream

Angels on Horseback

*Can be prepared in the
morning; broil just before serving.*

24 large plump oysters
(chicken livers or
mushrooms can be
substituted)
2 tablespoons paprika

¼ cup minced onion
12 slices of meaty bacon
24 toothpicks
1 tablespoon oil

Preheat broiler. Trim and beard the oysters, drain them, and pat dry with a towel. Combine paprika and onion and roll each oyster in the mixture. Cut each bacon slice into halves, and wrap each oyster in a piece of bacon; secure with a toothpick. Place oysters in a single layer on an oiled broiler pan and broil until bacon is crisp.

Garlic Herb Bread

4 ounces butter
1 large garlic clove
1 tablespoon paprika
¼ cup minced fresh parsley
¼ cup minced fresh basil

1 tablespoon crumbled dried
orégano
2 medium-size loaves of
French bread

Melt the butter in a small saucepan. Peel garlic and put through a press into the butter. Add paprika and herbs. Set aside for flavors to marry. Cut bread almost all the way through to the bottom, making 1¼-inch slices. Dip a pastry brush into the herb butter and brush bread slices on both sides. Place the loaves on a baking sheet and heat, uncovered, in a 350°F oven for 10 minutes. Serve hot.

Fresh Tomato Soup

*Can be prepared up to 2
days ahead.*

4 slices of bacon
2 large sweet onions
8 red-ripe tomatoes
2 tablespoons tomato
   ketchup
2 tablespoons flour
2 quarts chicken stock

2 tablespoons chopped fresh
   parsley
2 tablespoons chopped fresh
   basil
salt and pepper
Herb Croutons (recipe
   follows)

Herb Croutons

*Can be prepared up to 2 days
ahead; store in an airtight container.*

2 slices of bread
1 ounce butter

2 tablespoons chopped fresh
   parsley
2 tablespoons chopped fresh basil

Chop the bacon. Peel and slice the onions. Peel and chop tomatoes. Heat bacon pieces in a heavy-bottomed sauté pan and cook until bacon is just turning crisp and brown. Drain off all but 1 tablespoon of the fat, but leave the bacon in the pan. Add onions and sauté them with the bacon for 3 to 5 minutes, stirring frequently; do not burn the onions. Pour bacon-onion mixture into a large saucepan, at least 4-quart size, and add tomatoes, ketchup and flour. Stir well to incorporate flour in the tomato mixture. Add stock and herbs and bring to a boil. Reduce heat, cover, and simmer gently for 30 minutes. Taste and correct seasoning with salt and pepper if necessary. The soup may be puréed in a blender or can be served as is. Serve soup garnished with herb croutons.

Cut the bread into cubes. Melt the butter in a sauté pan and stir in bread cubes and herbs. Cook, stirring frequently, until croutons are slightly browned.

Red Pepper, Chick-pea and Romaine Salad

*Arrange and refrigerate salad ingredients
1 hour before the party.
Dress salad just before serving.*

1 large or 2 medium-size
   heads of romaine lettuce
4 cups cooked chick-peas

2 large red bell peppers
   Creamy Mustard Dressing
   (recipe follows)

Wash and dry romaine and separate the leaves. Tear the leaves into bite-size pieces and roll in a towel to store until ready to mix the salad. Place chick-peas in a colander and drain thoroughly. Set aside. Broil the peppers or roast in a 500°F oven. Turn peppers until skin is blistered on all sides. Place peppers in a paper bag, seal, and let them steam for 20 minutes. Then peel peppers, remove stems, ribs and seeds, and cut into thin slices. Set aside.

Combine romaine, chick-peas and red pepper strips no more than 1 hour before serving time. Chill until just before dinner, then leave at room temperature for about 30 minutes. Just before serving, pour on the dressing and toss to mix.

Creamy Mustard Dressing

Can be prepared 1 day ahead.

2 hard-cooked eggs
1 garlic clove
1½ teaspoons salt
1½ teaspoons sugar
1 teaspoon coarse-ground
   black pepper

1 tablespoon minced parsley
1 tablespoon prepared
   Dijon-style mustard
½ cup olive oil
5 tablespoons heavy cream
¼ cup wine vinegar

Peel and mash the eggs. Peel and mince the garlic. Combine eggs and garlic with all other dressing ingredients and stir well to mix. Makes about 1¼ cups dressing.

Broiled Flank Steak with Dry Marinade

1 flank steak, 4 to 5 pounds, about 1 inch thick	¼ cup vegetable oil

Dry Marinade

¼ cup sugar	3 tablespoons paprika
1 tablespoon salt	1 tablespoon garlic powder
1½ tablespoons black pepper	

Place steak in a shallow oblong dish. Combine marinade ingredients and pat on both sides of the meat, rubbing in well. Cover and refrigerate for 1½ to 2 hours.

Preheat broiler, or start charcoal fire, about 20 minutes before you plan to start broiling. Remove meat from the dish and shake off excess marinade. Brush steak with oil on both sides. Broil 3 to 4 inches from the heat source for about 4 minutes on each side for rare, or longer according to taste.

Country Apple Cake

Can be prepared 1 day ahead.

2 eggs	1 teaspoon ground cinnamon
2 cups sugar	½ teaspoon salt
½ cup vegetable oil	4 cups diced apples
2 cups sifted flour	1 cup chopped walnuts
2 teaspoons baking soda	½ teaspoon vanilla extract

Preheat oven to 350°F. Butter and flour a 10-inch bundt pan. In a large mixing bowl combine eggs and sugar and beat until lemon-colored and thick. Add oil, flour, baking soda, cinnamon and salt, and stir until well blended. Add apples, walnuts and vanilla, and stir again. Pour batter into the prepared pan. Bake in the oven for 50 to 60 minutes, or until a cake tester inserted in the center comes out dry and hot. Remove from the pan and cool.

Serve cake with vanilla ice cream, sprinkled with additional cinnamon if desired.

INDEX

Agurkesalat (Danish Cucumber Salad), 74
Alfalfa Sprouts, 61
Anise Butter, 38
Apple Salad with Watercress and Radishes, 75
Applesauce Spice Cakes, 98
Apricot Fruitcake, 99
Arugula, 57
Asinan (Balinese Green Salad), 77
Avgolemono (Greek Egg and Lemon Soup), 17
Avocado, 62
   Dressing, 70
   Preparing, 62, 63

Balinese Green Salad (Asinan), 77
Basil and Garlic Paste (Pistou), 16
Beans, (for salads), 63
Beans, Dried (for soups), 12, 13
Bean Sprouts, 63
Beef
   Chateaubriand with Duchesse Potatoes, 43
   Consommé, Clarified (Consommé Double), 10
   Cuts for Broiling, 30, 31
   Entrecôtes à la Bretonne, 44
   Filet Mignon with Blue Cheese, 42
   Flank Steak with Dry Marinade, Broiled, 109
   Soup with Herb Dumplings, 22
   Steak, Marinated, Florentine Style (Bistecca alla Fiorentina), 44
   Tournedos, Broiling, 31
Belgian Endive, 57
Bibb Lettuce, 57
Billi-Bi (Mussel Soup), 19
Bistecca alla Fiorentina (Marinated Steak, Florentine Style), 44
Blue Cheese Butter, 38
Blue Cheese Dressing, 68
Boston Lettuce, 57
Bouquet Garni, 4
Bread, Garlic Herb, 106
Broccoli, 63
Broiling, 30
   Chicken, 33
   Fish, 35
   Meat, 30, 31, 32
   Oven Broiling, General Tips, 30
   Poultry other than Chicken, 35
Brown Stock, 5
Butter Icing, 85, 86
Buttermilk Cucumber Dressing, 68
Butters, Compound, 37, 38
   Anise, 38
   Blue Cheese, 38
   Chive, 38
   Coriander, 38
   Curry, 38
   Garlic, 38
   Green Herb, 38
   Maître d'Hôtel, 37
   Mint, 38
   Mustard, 38
   Mustard-Watercress, 38
   Rosemary, 38
   Shellfish, 38

   Shrimp, 38
   Snail, 38
   Tarragon, 38
Butter-Sugar Filling, 95

Cabbage, 57
   and Apple Salad, 72
   and Pepper Salad, 74
   Coleslaw, 76
Cake(s), 82
   Apple, Country, 109
   Applesauce Spice, 98
   Chocolate, All-in-One, 96
   Cider, English, 98
   Devil's-Food, 94
   Flavoring, 82, 85
   Fruitcake, Apricot, 99
   Fruitcake, Scottish (Dundee Cake), 88–90
   Gingerbread Squares, 98
   Lemon, French (Gâteau au Citron), 97
   Madeira, 99
   One-Bowl, 84
   Pineapple Upside-Down, 100
   Poppy-Seed, 94
   Preparing a Deep Pan, 83
   Preparing a Layer Cake Pan, 83
   Seedcake, Cornish, 96
   Slicing a Deep Cake into Halves, 85
   Storage and Freezing, 85
   Variations, 82
   Walnut Layer, 100
Carrot(s), 62
   Preparing, 63
   and Watercress Soup, 20
Cauliflower, 63
Celery and Walnut Soup, 21
Celery Knob, 63
Charlotte, Strawberry, Malakoff, 92
Chicken
   Broiled, Dijonnaise, 48
   Broiling, 33
   Butterflying, 33
   Cock-a-Leekie, 21
   Country-Style, 47
   Cutting Parts, 36
   Deviled, 48
   and Mushroom Soup, Oriental, 18
   in Spicy Tomato Sauce, 48
   Stock, 14
   Tandoori-Style, 46
   with Lemon Marinade, Broiled, 47
Chick-pea
   and Spinach Salad with Yogurt, 72
   Red Pepper, Chick-pea and Romaine Salad, 108
   Soup, Tunisian, 29
Chicory, 57
Chinese Cabbage, 57, 58
Chinese Hot and Sour Soup, 23
Chive Butter, 38
Chocolate
   Butter Frosting, 95
   Cake, All-in-One, 96

Cream Frosting, 96
Cider Cake, English, 98
Cock-a-Leekie, 21
Coffee Essence, Note, 82, 100
Coleslaw, 76
Compound Butters, 37, 38
Confectioners' Sugar Icing, 85, 86
Consommé, *see* Soup
Coriander Butter, 38
Cornish Seedcake, 96
Country Apple Cake, 109
Croutons, 13
Croutons, Herb, 107
Cucumber, 63
    Preparing, 63
    Salad, Danish (Agurkesalat), 74
Curry Butter, 38

Dandelion and Bacon Salad, 77
Danish Cucumber Salad (Agurkesalat), 74
Devil's-Food Cake, 94
Dicing, 64
Dumplings, Herb, 22
Dundee Cake (Scottish Fruitcake), 88–90

English Cider Cake, 98
English Salad Cream, 68
Escarole, 58

Fennel, 62
    Preparing, 63
Filling, Butter-Sugar, 95
Fish
    Broiling, 35
    Filleting, Boning and Skinning, 34
    fumet, 7
    Roes, Broiling, 35
    Stock, 7, 14
    See also names of fish
French Lemon Cake (Gâteau au Citron), 97
French Onion Soup, 24
Frosting and Icing
    Butter Icing, 85, 86
    Chocolate Butter Frosting, 95
    Chocolate Cream Frosting, 96
    Confectioners' Sugar Icing, 85, 86
    flavoring, 82, 85
    Vanilla Frosting, 94

Garlic
    Butter, 38
    for salads, 59, 60
    Herb Bread, 106
    Using, 60
Garnishes, 65, 66–67
    Brushes or Fringes, 65, 66
    Chiffonade, 65
    Chrysanthemums, 65, 66
    Curls, 65, 66
    Julienne Strips, 65
    Mushrooms, Turned, 67
    Roses, 65
    Shapes, 65, 67
    Skewered Tidbits, 65
Gâteau au Citron (French Lemon Cake), 97
Gingerbread Squares, 98
Grapefruit and Sesame Salad, 73
Greek Egg and Lemon Soup (Avgolemono), 17
Gruyère and Mushroom Salad, 77

Herb(s)
    Croutons, 107
    Dumplings, 22
    Green Herb Butter, 38
    for salads, 60
Hot and Sour Soup, Chinese, 23

Iceberg Lettuce, 58
Icing a Cake, 86
Icings, *see* Frosting and Icing

Julienne, 64

Lamb
    Chops with Mint, Turkish Style, 45
    Cuts for Broiling, 32, 33
    Leg of, Butterflied, with Vodka Sauce, 44
    Rack of, with Tomatoes, 45
Lamb's Lettuce, 54, 58
Leaf Lettuce, 58
Leek Soup, 25
Lemon Juice for salads, 60
Lemon Marinade, 47

Mackerel, Split, Broiled, 49
Madeira Cake, 99
Maître d'Hôtel Butter, 38
Maple Syrup Icing, 88
Marinade
    Classic, 30
    Dry, 109
    Lemon, 47
Marmalade Dressing, 69
Meat, Broiling, 30, 31, 32
    See also names of meat
Menu: Harvest Dinner, 104
Meringue Frosting, 87
Mincing, 64, 65
Mint Butter, 38
Mushrooms, 63
Mussel Soup (Billi-Bi), 19
Mustard
    Butter, 38
    Dressing, Creamy, 108
    for salads, 60
    Watercress Butter, 38

Nasturtium, 59

Oil for salads, 59
One-Bowl Cake, 84
Onions, 63
Onion Soup, French, 24
Orange and Olive Salad, 74
Orange and Tomato Soup, 25
Oriental Chicken and Mushroom Soup, 18
Oysters, Angels on Horseback, 106

Peas, 63
Pepper *(Nigrum)*, for salads, 60
Peppers *(Capsicum)*, 63
    Red Pepper, Chick-pea and Romaine Salad, 108
Pineapple Upside-Down Cake, 101
Pistou (Basil and Garlic Paste), 16
Poppy-Seed Cake, 94
Pork
    Chops, Broiling, 32

Pork (*continued*)
    Chops, Country-Style, 42
    Chops, Smoked, with Mustard, 42
    Cuts for Broiling, 32
    Loin Chops with Sauce Robert, 38, 40–41
Potatoes Duchesse, 43
Poultry, Broiling, 33
    See also Chicken
Processor Shredding, 64
Provençal Vegetable Soup (Soupe au Pistou), 16
Puréeing Vegetable Soups, 12

Radishes, 63
Romaine, 58
Rosemary Butter, 38

Salad(s)
    Apple, with Watercress and Radishes, 75
    Assembling, 57, 61
    Cabbage and Apple, 72
    Cabbage and Pepper, 74
    Chick-pea and Spinach, with Yogurt, 72
    Coleslaw, 76
    Cucumber, Danish (Agurkesalat), 74
    Dandelion and Bacon, 77
    Grapefruit and Sesame, 73
    Green, Balinese (Asinan), 77
    Green, Italian, 71
    Green (Salade Verte), 70
    Greens, 57
    Greens, Preparing, 58, 59, 61
    Gruyère and Mushroom, 77
    Orange and Olive, 74
    Red Pepper, Chick-pea and Romaine, 108
    Spinach and Cheese, 72
    Vegetable Ingredients, Preparing, 61, 62
Salad Dressing, 59
    Avocado, 63, 70
    Blue Cheese, 68
    Buttermilk Cucumber, 68
    English Salad Cream, 68
    Marmalade, 69
    Mustard, Creamy, 108
    Sweet-and-Sour, 69
    Tahini, 68
    Tarragon Cream, 70
    Tomato Sour-Cream, 69
    Vinaigrette, 60
    Yogurt and Honey, 69
Salmon Steaks, Florentine, 50
Salt for Salads, 60
Sauce
    Demi-glace, 38
    Robert, 38
    Tomato, Spicy, 48
    Vodka, 44
Scallions for salads, 60
Scallops, Broiled, 51
Scotch Broth, 16
Scottish Fruitcake (Dundee Cake), 88–90
Shallots for salads, 60
Shellfish Butter, 38
Shrimp Butter, 38
Slicing and Chopping, 64
Snail Butter, 38
Sorrel, 59
Soup(s)
    Beef, with Herb Dumplings, 22
    Carrot and Watercress, 20
    Celery and Walnut, 21
    Chicken and Mushroom, Oriental, 18

    Chick-pea, Tunisian, 19
    Cock-a-Leekie, 21
    Consommé, 9, 11
    Consommé, Beef, Clarified (Consommé Double), 10
    Consommé Rosé, 15
    Egg and Lemon, Greek (Avgolemono), 17
    Garnishing, 13
    Hearty Broths, 9
    Hot and Sour, Chinese, 23
    Leek, 25
    Mussel (Billi-Bi), 19
    Onion, French, 24
    Orange and Tomato, 25
    Puréed Soups, 11–12
    Scotch Broth, 16
    Stracciatella, 18
    Tomato, Fresh, 107
    Vegetable, Provençal (Soupe au Pistou), 16
    Vegetable, Puréeing, 12
    Zuppa alla Pavese, 20
Soupe au Pistou (Provençal Vegetable Soup), 16
Spinach, 59, 95
Spinach and Cheese Salad, 72
Stock, 4
    Brown, 5
    Chicken, 14
    Fish, 7, 14
    Preparing Ingredients, 4–5
    Reducing to concentrate flavor, 7
    Storing, 9
    Straining, 7
    Vegetable, 14
    White, 6
Stracciatella, 18
Strawberry Charlotte Malakoff, 91–93
Striped Bass, Broiled, with Fennel, 49
Sugar Decorations for cakes, 86
Sweet-and-Sour Dressing, 69
Swordfish, Broiled, 51

Tahini Dressing, 68
Tarragon Butter, 38
Tarragon Cream Dressing, 70
Tomato(es), 63
    Preparing, 62
    Soup, Fresh, 107
    Sour-Cream Dressing, 69
Tunisian Chick-pea Soup, 19

Vanilla Frosting, 94
Vegetable(s)
    For salads, 61
    Preparing, 62–63
    Soup, Puréeing, 12
    Stock, 14
    See also names of vegetables
Vinaigrette Dressing, 60
Vinegar for salads, 60

Walnut Layer Cake, 100
Watercress, 59
White Stock, 6
Wine: Zinfandel, 105

Yogurt and Honey Dressing, 69

Zucchini, 63
Zuppa alla Pavese, 20